Katherine A Clarke

Lyrical Echoes

Katherine A Clarke

Lyrical Echoes

ISBN/EAN: 9783744772013

Printed in Europe, USA, Canada, Australia, Japan

Cover: Foto ©ninafisch / pixelio.de

More available books at **www.hansebooks.com**

BY

KATHERINE A. CLARKE

TORONTO:
WILLIAM BRIGGS
Wesley Buildings
1899

Entered according to Act of the Parliament of Canada, in the year one thousand eight hundred and ninety-nine, by WILLIAM BRIGGS, at the Department of Agriculture.

CONTENTS.

	PAGE
The Union Jack	9
A Question	10
Post Mortem Love	11
Lost Years	13
Affliction	14
A Kiss	15
A Wife's Reverie	16
Palestine	18
True Valuation	20
Memories	21
Widmer Hall	22
"I Change Not"	24
Pleasure—Pain	28
Childhood	29
Blessings	29
Speak No Evil	30
Longings	31
Troubles	31
Toronto	32
When Things Go Wrong	32
Waiting	33
Trifles	34
"Our Father"	35
Heaven	37
Trust	38

CONTENTS.

	PAGE
A Christmas Carol	39
"A City Whose Builder and Maker is God"	41
A Water-Lily	43
Ambition	44
Victoria Regina	45
Happiness	46
A Jubilee Prayer	47
Woman	49
Old Songs, Old Flowers	51
My Fortune	52
Beauty	52
Charity	53
Friendship	54
The Christian's Belief	54
The Past	55
Time	56
A Word	57
The Poet	58
Canada	59
Retrospect	61
Death	62
"Who Lovéd Me"	63
To-Day	65
"Gloria in Excelsis Deo"	66
"Till the Day Break"	67
Rest	68
"Love Never Faileth"	68
Wishes	69
My Beloved	70
"Do Noble Deeds, not Dream Them all Day Long"	71
"Why Stand Ye Here all the Day Idle?"	73
Little Things	74
Advice	75
Unsatisfied	76
Afterwards	77

CONTENTS.

	PAGE
Compensation	78
"Love Begets Love"	78
A Funeral	79
Easter Sunday	80
"Go Ye into all the World and Preach the Gospel"	81
"Without Shedding of Blood is no Remission"	83
"Thy Will be Done"	84
"Rest in the Lord"	85
Thanksgiving Day	87
The Apostles' Creed	88
Nothing	89
"The Lord is my Shepherd"	90
Truth	91
No Room	93
A Legend	94
Procrastination	95
If We Had Known	96
Duty	97
Gray Hairs	98
The Sparrow	99
A Boy	100
Love	101
"He Knoweth Our Frame"	102
Pain	103
Christmas Morning	104
The Word	105
Safety	106
"A Little While"	107
Riches	108
Old Ocean	109
Spring	111
A Birthday Wish	111
Snow	112
Take the Sweet	113
Winter	114

CONTENTS.

	PAGE
"Suffer and Be Strong"	115
A Fable	116
"Be Thou Faithful"	117
Lines on the Death of a Little Girl	118
Life's Sea	119
In Memoriam	120
To a Little Girl on her First Christmas	121
Lines to a Young Lady on her Wedding Day	123
Eternity	124
A Modern Satire	125
Disciples	126
Cupid	127
"The Greatest of These is Love"	128
Christmas	129
Faith	129
Christ	130
Only	130
"Time Enough"	131
Greatness	132
He Leadeth	132
My Ship	133
Silence	134
Faithful	134
A Query	135
Christ's Coming	136
Vanity	136
The Christian Walk	137
The Bible	138
The Gospel	139
Prayer	139
Mary and Martha	140
"He that Regardeth the Clouds shall not Reap"	141
His Banner	142
"Without Me ye can do nothing"	143
"What shall I ask?"	144

CONTENTS.

	PAGE
"Ye are My Witnesses"	146
Patience and Perseverance	146
Anticipation	147
Home	148
Look on the Bright Side	149
A Patchwork Quilt	150
A Birthday	151
Life	152
Abiding Places	152
The Old Year	153
"Beauty is Vain"	154
Disguised Blessings	155
Nobility	156
Complaint	157

LYRICAL ECHOES.

THE UNION JACK.

Ever victorious
   Over the world;
Honour it, stick to it,
   Keep it unfurled.
It shall not be beaten,
   Around it we'll stand,
The flag of our fathers,
   Our Queen and our land!

For centuries nobly
   It's floated on high,
O'er earth and on ocean,
   Against the blue sky.
True soldiers and sailors
   It never shall lack;
Our country's dear banner,
   The old Union Jack!

A QUESTION.

"How much do I love you?" I'll tell you when you
    Have explained all the system above—
The sun and the moon, comets, meteors, and stars—
    All upheld by an infinite love;
The day and the night, and the shine and the storm,
    For centuries ever controlled;
Seedtime and harvest and summer and snow,
    Each in time and in season unrolled.

"How much do I love you?" I'll tell you when you
    Have fathomed the sea with a measure,
When you've solved all the wonders concerning the world,
    And sought for and found all her treasure;
Unravelled the mysteries of light and of heat,
    Electricity, science, and lore,
Given me the date of the birth of the earth,
    And the marvels that happened of yore.

"How much do I love you?" You surely ere this
    Have read my reply in your heart.
You can't answer my questions; no more can I yours,
    For my love is not measure nor part:
I love you, I know, but I can't say how much;
    I'm yours only, forever and all—
Tongue or pen cannot reckon the wealth of a heart
    Once surendered at love's gracious call.

POST MORTEM LOVE.

AND is this dying?
So calmly lying;
No pain, no sighing
   Can touch her now;
Nor woe nor weeping,
So sweetly sleeping,
Death's angel keeping
   Her pallid brow.

Her worth they measure
By sorrow's leisure,
And flowery treasure
   To deck her frame;
Sweet tributes bringing,
Her praises singing,
Her honour ringing,
   They crown her name.

Kind thoughts upwelling,
Her goodness telling
As in her dwelling
   She lies in state;
Regards they tender,
Rich flowers they send her,
And love's grace lend her,
   When 'tis too late.

POST MORTEM LOVE.

Oh! friend or lover,
When my life's over
I ask not cover
   Of silk and flowers;
'Tis now I'm needing
The kind God-speeding,
The heart's true reading
   For living hours.

The graceful token,
The kind word spoken,
The vows unbroken,
   Will gild the tomb;
And sad bereaving
Lose half its grieving,
If love is weaving
   Its light in gloom.

Life soon is ending;
Give now the tending,
Love and befriending,
   Doubt not nor wait;
For many a parting
Will owe its smarting
And tears upstarting
   To love too late,

LOST YEARS.

> "We always may be what we might have been."
> —Adelaide Procter.

"We always may be what we might have been,"—
These words look true upon the surface seen,
But, read beneath the lines, though fair it seem,
'Tis a fool's paradise, youth's idle dream;
The life we've lost we never can redeem.

We dally in the glowing morn of youth,
Play battledore and shuttlecock with truth,
And waste bright days, then sadly amid fears
The training lost mourn o'er with bitter tears;
But wisdom's offers go with passing years.

The ways of sin we tread, and oft return;
A better path, a nobler life we yearn,
Regret the past, claim pardon in Christ's name,
But bygone purity can ne'er reclaim;
The hand that sows "wild oats" must reap the same.

The noble vessel with the billows tost,
Her anchor, rudder, sails, and compass lost,
May in a day of calm seas reach the shore
A battered wreck, not glorious as of yore—
Safe home, but beauty gone for evermore.

The fallen blossom ne'er will fruit attain;
The moments flown we never can regain;
The golden hours with glorious chances teem,
The past is gone, the future but a dream;
Then haste, awake, the fleeting years redeem.

Ghosts of the past, appearing weird and lean,
Show in derision what we might have been.
God may, in mercy, blot out the old score,
But chances gone no power can e'er restore;
The time once lost is lost for evermore.

AFFLICTION.

In the furnace of affliction
   With its testing and its gloom,
Sorrows bring a benediction,
   Graces take a sweeter bloom.

In the furnace of affliction
   Holiest pleasures oft are found;
Peace beyond earth's contradiction,
   Faith and hope and love abound.

In the furnace of affliction
   Souls are purged from sin and dross,
Soon in God's own jurisdiction
   Crown to wear instead of cross.

A KISS.

What is a kiss? Something better than money,
Dearer than praises and sweeter than honey;
Oldest and best of all earth's nectared wine,
Love's own exclusive, appropriate sign.

'Tis Cupid's quaint language, when he, condescending
To earth, keeps the bounds of his kingdom extending;
'Tis a shaft from his quiver that carries no sting,
A touch of his raiment, a brush of his wing.

'Tis his oath of allegiance, both binding and tender,
The seal of his subjects' completest surrender;
A pledge for the Future, a gleam from the Past,
An emblem of Love that forever will last.

'Tis peculiar to all, earth's distinctions effacing,
The lips' silent speech, the divinest embracing,
The fondest expression, the perfection of bliss—
All this and much more may be found in a kiss.

A WIFE'S REVERIE.

How oft do I remember
A certain bleak December,
When the firelight's fitful ember
   Cast its shadow on the wall!
And strange figures weird and wizened
In the glowing gloom soon glistened,
'Twas there I sat and listened
   To your heart's loving call.

I tasted then a sweetness,
A measure of completeness
That gives this life its meetness,
   Makes poverty rich store;
True words a dear voice ringing,
Rich adoration bringing,
Music surpassing singing
   I e'er had heard before.

Eden's first story telling,
Its freshness still upwelling,
Two hearts once more were swelling,
   Past loneliness was done;
United lives then making,
Old ties and interests breaking,
All other loves forsaking,
   Cleave only unto one.

A WIFE'S REVERIE.

Your homage true and tender
Was pledged as my defender;
Your spirit did engender
   New life and joy in mine;
I needed not long pressing,
My love for thee confessing,
To gladly put, caressing,
   My hand, my all, in thine.

Wife, mother now, not maiden,
Rich life with treasure laden,
A sort of blissful Aidenn
   Of earth's and heaven's cheer;
The golden bells still pealing,
Their echoes onward stealing,
Sweet harmony revealing
   A taste of glory here.

So, closer we are growing,
Each other better knowing,
Together upward going
   To the fair home above;
But I will aye remember
That day in bleak December,
When, by the firelight's ember,
   You told me of your love.

PALESTINE.

Oh, Palestine! oh, Palestine!
   My heart oft turns to thee;
Thou art the Lord's own chosen land,
   And destined great to be.

The smallest, yet the holiest place
   Of all the mighty earth,
Thy chronicles alone record
   A Saviour's humble birth.

Thy Maker stood upon thy shores,
   Thy fields are holy ground,
Thy lakes and hills are sacred now,
   With precious memories bound.

Thy walls and stones, thy fruits and flowers
   Formed topic for His speech;
Cities and valleys, plains and streams
   Eternal lessons teach.

Thy poor were sought, thy children taught,
   Thy hungry ones were fed,
Blind found their sight, the dumb their tongue,
   To life were raised thy dead.

Thy sin and strife, thy troubled life
  Thy Sovereign came to heal;
What richer gift, what loftier joy
  Could earthly kingdom feel?

A Saviour walking on thy sod,
  Alas, for human pride!
What lower depth could mortal fall?
  That Saviour crucified!

It was unto His own He came;
  He wept, thy peace He yearned;
Thy rulers gave Him felon's death,
  And His salvation spurned.

Oh, Palestine! oh, Palestine!
  Thou art forsaken now;
God took the sceptre from thy hand,
  The crown from off thy brow.

Thy children now are scattered far,
  A wandering, alien band;
A land without a people mourns
  A people without land.

When He arrived in lowliness
  Thou didst reject thy King;
And now alone thou weepest sore,
  Thy funeral dirges sing.

Oh, Palestine! oh, Palestine!
  Thy God will come again
As "King of kings" and "Lord of lords,"
  With judgment in His train.

Then thou, dear land, shall rise again,
  In exaltation be,
Thy King be glorious o'er the world,
  His sway from sea to sea.

TRUE VALUATION.

"The rank is but the guinea stamp,
* The man alone the sterling gold."*
            —Burns.

We no longer value a man for his wealth,
  Nor despise him because he is poor,
We worship him not for his beauty or health,
  Nor do his possessions allure.
We honour him not for his land or his name,
  The pleasures or gains that await,
Nor for his position, nor yet for his fame,
  Nor his title to noble estate.
We value a man for just what he is worth—
  Young, fortunate, lowly, or old—
These trifles are only the stamp of the earth,
  The man is the genuine gold.

MEMORIES.

The rain is falling, and voices calling
   Have carried us back to the days of yore,
Like sweet bells pealing, their echoes stealing
   The memory of hours that shall come no more.

Alone in the gloaming we hear them roaming,
   Those gentle ghosts from the land of dreams;
Still closer pressing, they come confessing
   The golden glamour of bygone gleams.

Aside we're turning, the past years yearning,
   The joy, the trouble, despair or gloom,
To-day forgetting our sun is setting
   In darkest night in the past's old tomb.

Laughing or weeping, past vigils keeping,
   Communing alone with the ghosts of the dead;
Unheeding to-morrow we mourn in sorrow,
   While the raindrops patter above our head.

WIDMER HALL.

I RETURNED in fact and fancy
   To my childhood's happy home,
And from attic down to cellar
   Trod where I was wont to roam.
Bare, untidy, and forsaken,
   The old house now lonely stands;
Weeds and spiders climb where roses
   Once were trained by careful hands.

The old house, and yet so different,
   Scarce, methinks, it is the same,
'Tis like many a time-scarred veteran
   Who has long outlived his fame.
Kitchen garden, lawn, and orchard,
   All are lost in business sway,
And where little feet once wandered
   Factories toil and smoke to-day.

The old well that used to offer
   Crystal water pure and sweet;
The low apple-tree whose shadow
   Formed an often sought retreat;
Trees beneath whose leafy shelter
   Built we castles in the air—
Looking out of childhood's vision
   All the world appears so fair—

These are gone ; the old house only
   Silent stands amid the din
Of the busy life about it,
   With its records sealed within.
Three generations claimed its shelter,
   Fondly called the old place home ;
Some are in the land celestial,
   Others lands terrestrial roam.

Years roll backward as I wander
   O'er the days and things of yore,
And from out the past's rich treasure
   Gather good for future store.
Ah! the years are gone forever,
   Yet we call them back at will ;
Like a dream when one awaketh,
   They shall live in memory still.

All our earthly homes may perish,
   Echoes of a vanished past ;
Let them teach us still to cherish
   Better things that ever last ;
For somewhere on God's horizon,
   Far beyond our mortal ken,
Is a home of "many mansions,"
   Jesus has prepared for men.

"I CHANGE NOT."

Malachi iii. 6.

"I change not!" "I change not!"
   Though earth's treasures rust,
Its pleasures be labelled
   "From dust unto dust."
Its silver may tarnish,
   Its fine gold grow dim,
Its joy cup with sorrow
   Be filled to the brim;
Its peace may be broken,
   Its beauty may fade,
Its true worth and honour
   Be cast in the shade;
Its friendships be riven,
   And fleeting its fame,
Yet Jesus, our Jesus
   Is ever the same.

"I change not!" "I change not!"
   Though riches may fly,
Though dangers be thickening
   And poverty nigh;
Though rags take the place
   Of purple and white,
Tears succeed singing,
   And day change to night;

"I CHANGE NOT."

Pain follow rejoicing,
   And famine the feast,
(For the world gives the most
   When 'tis needed the least);
Though men may erase
   From earth's tablet our name,
Yet Jesus, our Jesus
   Is ever the same.

"I change not!" "I change not!"
   Though business may change,
And things we once managed
   Another arrange;
Our wishes neglected,
   Opinions unsought,
Our help undervalued
   Or counted as naught;
Though others take places
   Once reckoned as ours,
And leave us the thorns,
   While they gather the flowers
Life at best is uncertain,
   Then greater good claim,
For our King and His business
   Are ever the same.

"I change not!" "I change not!"
   Though changing earth's fame,
Its time-honoured titles
   Be trampled in shame.

"I CHANGE NOT."

The applause of this world
  Is as brief as its night,
It calls evil good,
  And the wrong-doer right;
Its best adoration
  Will soon pass away,
For its wreaths are but laurel,
  And fade in a day.
Seek lofty ambition,
  True worth, a great name,
Joint heir with a Sovereign
  Who's ever the same.

"I change not!" "I change not!"
  Though health may depart,
The spring from the step,
  And the life from the heart.
The light of the eyes
  May grow feeble and dim,
But faith's perfect vision
  Can gaze upon Him.
The ear may get deaf,
  And the tongue may be tied,
And all that is purest
  Or sweetest denied;
Yet still it holds true
  (Though the world counts it strange),
The believer is happy,
  For God cannot change.

"I CHANGE NOT."

"I change not!" "I change not!"
   Though friends may all change,
Time's messengers carry them
   Out of our range;
The hands oft extended
   May seek ours no more;
Where once waited welcome
   We see a closed door;
Though lips that our praises
   So lavishly sing,
Through misunderstanding
   Our loving hearts sting;
Though death may remove them,
   Or foes may estrange,
Yet God is our Friend,
   And He never can change.

"I change not!" "I change not!"
   Though seasons may wane,
The summer turn winter,
   The sunshine prove rain,
The noonday be followed
   By darkness of night,
And we walk in the shadow
   Instead of the light;
Vine and fig-tree be barren,
   Yea, no fruit at all,
The fields yield no crop,
   And no herd in the stall;

Though all earth should fail us,
  We'll joy in His name,
For Jesus, our Jesus
  Is ever the same.

"I change not!" "I change not!"
  Though all else decay,
The mountains be levelled,
  The sea pass away;
The elements melt
  At the touch of His breath,
The universe stilled
  In the silence of death;
The heavens as parchment
  Together be rolled,
The stars fall from orbits
  They've travelled of old;
But nothing can shake
  The foundation we claim,
For Jesus, Jehovah
  Is ever the same.

PLEASURE — PAIN.

Like a dream, e'en gone to-morrow,
  Months of pleasure swiftly fly,
While each day of pain or sorrow
  Like an age creeps slowly by.

CHILDHOOD.

I sit in the garden beside the sweet blossoms,
  Or lie 'neath the shade of the old apple tree,
Forgetting the present, I dream of the future,
  And wonder and wonder what my life will be—
      Hours with love laden?
      A bright, happy maiden?
  Come, fairies, and tell it to me.

Oh! will it be joyful, or will it be gloomy?
  Fraught with earth's sorrows, or blest with its peace?
Hasten, slow years, I am longing to read it,
  Bring to me pleasures that never shall cease;
      Love, pain, or glory?
      Oh! what is my story?
  Come, fairies, and tell it to me.

BLESSINGS.

We value not the priceless boon of health
  Till the dread hand of pain has laid us low;
We do not prize the blessedness of wealth
  Till we have lost the power it can bestow.
We do not cherish life and love and friends
  Until Death's fingers break the golden strings;
We're not half grateful for the gifts God sends—
  We miss our blessings when they've taken wings.

SPEAK NO EVIL.

Oh, breathe no ill of others' lives,
    Or in such converse bear a part ;
Words can give sorer wounds than knives,
    And sadly lacerate the heart.
Judge not, oh, man, thy fellow-man,
    Leave that to Him who reads the mind,
But search for all the good you can,
    For they who seek shall surely find.

Be tender in your speech of all,
    And never let your voice be heard
Condemning others for their fall,
    Or slandering them by deed or word.
To others' failings close your eyes,
    And tarnish not another's name,
For who shall say that you would rise
    A better man if tried the same.

Then lenient be to others' faults,
    As you would have them be to you,
And take no part in those assaults
    That taint the noble and the true.
For God alone can judge the man,
    And we must all before Him stand ;
Then ever speak the best you can,
    And reach to all a helping hand.

LONGINGS.

When we are but children, we long and we cry
   For youth and for liberty's power;
When that has arrived, then for manhood we sigh,
   Its dignity, knowledge, or dower.

When we have attained the position or chance,
   The profession or business we love,
It straightway awakes a desire to advance,
   We seek for another above.

Gold added to silver and honor to name,
   Of lands and possessions a store,
We are not contented; the longing for fame
   Prompts us to accumulate more.

And thus it is ever; both early and late,
   We're subject to Fortune's frail wand;
We have and we hold, and we work and we wait,
   But we're looking for something beyond.

TROUBLES.

We laugh at past trouble and care,
   The present we hope to survive;
But the troubles the hardest to bear
   Are the troubles that never arrive.

TORONTO.

Queen City, hail! we homage pay,
    Thine happy sons and daughters;
Queen of the West, thou holdest sway
    O'er blue Ontario's waters.
We love thy streets, thy parks, thy streams;
    Thy life and homes we cherish;
They linger long in memory's dreams,
    Though other visions perish.
Pleasure be thine, and wealth, and calm,
    The brightest and the best;
Strive on, and win the highest palm,
    Queen City of the West!

WHEN THINGS GO WRONG.

When everything seems going wrong,
    And cares and griefs perplex us,
When tears will flow instead of song,
    And friends combine to vex us,
We should not moan, nor blame, nor curse,
    Nor sink our life in sorrow,
But say, "Thank God it is no worse,"
    And look for joy to-morrow.

WAITING.

WAITING is the hardest task
   In this busy world of ours ;
"Give us any work," we ask,
   Plucking thorns or culling flowers,
But, oh, tell us not to wait ;
   Hope deferred is bitter pain,
We are eager, and we hate
   Waiting on for bliss or bane.

Yes, 'tis hard, 'tis hard to wait !
   Body, spirit, mind rebel ;
And we find, alas, too late,
   We've not learned our lesson well !
The best fruits of earth are growing
   Where fair Patience guards the gate ;
He has found a truth worth knowing,
   Who has learned to calmly wait.

TRIFLES.

Only a smile, but it did wile
   Away a weary hour of pain;
Only a word, but she who heard
   The richer grew in hope and gain.
Only a touch, it was not much,
   Yet heart met heart in clasp of hand;
Only a kiss, yet memory's bliss
   Is treasured in a far-off land.
Such things are sweet; it is not meet
   That we of trifles misers grow;
We may not know the heaven below
   We make or mar for others so;
For after all, great things seem small,
   Small deeds are great if men be true.
Love brings no cost, is never lost;
   Love others, and they will love you.

"OUR FATHER."

"Our Father," dear Father,
   We come to Thee now,
And ask Thee to bless
   As at Thy throne we bow;
And teach us to hallow
   Thy wondrous name,
On earth as in heaven
   Its glory proclaim.

We ask Thee to hasten
   The glorious hour
When Thy Son in His beauty
   Shall rule here in power;
When earth to His footstool
   Her tribute shall bring,
And over all nations
   Our Lord shall be King.

And teach us, dear Father,
   To live in Thy will;
In all life's dark places
   To trust and be still.
So with faith in Thy guiding
   The crown shall be won,
And 'twill sweeten all sorrows
   If "Thy will be done."

"OUR FATHER."

We ask Thee to give us
   The blessings we need,
And out of Thy bounty
   Thy poor ones we'll feed;
Thy power will sustain us
   In sin's constant strife,
And day by day give us
   The true "Bread of Life."

Forgive us our trespasses,"
   Father, we pray,
As we forgive those
   Who have wronged us this day.
Make us tender-hearted,
   Forgiving, and kind,
Acting ever towards others
   With Thy loving mind.

Keep us from temptation,
   From wandering and sin;
"Deliver from evil"
   Without and within.
And teach us to walk
   In Thy life-giving light,
For "Thine is the kingdom,"
   The glory and might.

HEAVEN.

Somewhere, afar or near, on God's horizon
    There is a better land;
We know, we see it in the midnight watches,
    And on its threshold stand.

A home that has sweet welcome for the weary,
    Plenty, and peace, and mirth;
Its gain a compensation for all crosses
    That must be borne on earth.

A life where we shall find this life completed,
    And end the search for truth;
Our hopes, our aims, our joys, find richer promise
    Than the fond dreams of youth.

From daylight until dark we hear earth's calling
    To labour, love, and prayer;
From vesper hymn to matin song the music
    Of those who worship there.

This life is but the portal of the other,
    Where, perfect, we shall dwell
In bliss supreme and glory everlasting,
    Beyond man's power to tell.

TRUST.

Afar on the great roaring ocean
   A magnificent vessel was tost;
Amid the storm's blackest commotion
   And billows she well nigh was lost.
The artillery of heaven was crashing,
   With brightness that turned night to day,
The waves into wild fury lashing,
   As they closed in to swallow their prey.
The people on board her were shaking,
   Pallid, with sad thoughts of home;
The spirits of many were quaking
   With fears of the judgment to come.
But right in their midst sat a maiden
   Who of summers had seen half a score,
Her face bright, serene, and unladen,
   As if safe at her own cottage door.
"My little one," spake up a stranger,
   Yet voicing the question of all,
"This ship is in terrible danger,
   Do no fears your spirit appall?
Dread thoughts all our pleasures o'erwhelm."
   Then she turned, with a smile on her lip,
Saying, "My father's there at the helm,
   And he knows how to manage the ship."
The Lord give us more of her spirit
   In all earth's upheavals and strife,

A faith that rests not on our merit,
   But on Him who is guiding our life.
In smooth seas or rough no repining,
   No terror our souls to o'erwhelm;
Sweet trust, whether gloomy or shining,
   For our Father is holding the helm.

A CHRISTMAS CAROL.

Christmas morning, we hail thy dawning!
   The day of the birth of our Lord and King;
Hail victorious, crowned and glorious!
   Tributes and trophies to Him we bring.
        We'll tell the story,
        How heaven's glory
Shone over the darkness of Judah's plain;
        Our carols singing,
        Our offerings bringing
To Him who ever henceforth shall reign.

God's love professing, He came, earth's blessing,
   A helpless babe in a lonely inn;
"No room," a stranger, His bed a manger,
   The Child who can save the world from sin.
        We'll tell the story,
        How heaven's glory
Shone over the darkness of Judah's plain;

Our carols singing,
Our offerings bringing
To Him who ever henceforth shall reign.

Sinful, needing a Saviour's pleading,
   We'll chant with gladness that Saviour born;
While joy-bells ringing and children singing
   Proclaim to the world the Christmas morn.
We'll tell the story,
How heaven's glory
Shone over the darkness of Judah's plain;
Our carols singing,
Our offerings bringing
To Him who ever henceforth shall reign.

No longer tarry; the tidings carry,
   Till His flag is over the earth unfurled,
All seek His favour, and crown Him Saviour,
   For in His glory He'll rule the world.
We'll tell the story,
How heaven's glory
Shone over the darkness of Judah's plain;
Our carols singing,
Our offerings bringing
To Him who ever henceforth shall reign.

"A CITY WHOSE BUILDER AND MAKER IS GOD."

HEBREWS xi. 10.

THERE is a city, a beautiful city,
   Fairer and brighter than any we know,
Built by a Father, in infinite pity,
   For those of His children who wander below.
        And its bright beauty
        Owes not its duty
   To architects earthly, or wisdom of man;
        Pleasing and vernal,
        That city eternal
Traces its life to Omnipotent plan,

And in that city, that beautiful city,
   The walls are of gems and the streets are of gold;
There is no heat, and no cold, and no night-time,
   The residents never grow sickly or old.
        Pearl are the gates,
        And no spirit e'er waits,
   For the gates of the city are aye open wide;
        Angels are tending,
        And loving, befriending
The souls that the porter has ushered inside.

And in that city, that beautiful city,
   There windeth a river unceasing and clear;

And on each bank there are trees ever growing,
  All bearing fragrance, and healing, and cheer.
      Ever on flowing
      That river is going,
  Upward and onward to God's mighty throne;
      Souls here may sever,
      But at that fair river
  None are forsaken, or sad, or alone.

And in that city, that beautiful city,
  There is no temple—no need of one there—
For the inhabitants all are redeemed ones,
  Whom the Lord of the land for the place did prepare.
      No church, bell, or steeple,
      For there all the people
  In the beauty of holiness worship the King;
      And their glad story
      Of His great glory
  Makes all the arches with melody ring.

And in that city, that beautiful city,
  They need not the light of a candle or sun;
"Time is no more," for they measure not hourly—
  Years never begin there and never are done.
      No pleasures abating
      With watching and waiting,
  All present and lasting, the brightest and best;
      Not dying, but living,
      Eternity giving
  To mortals a palace, a crown, and a rest.

And in that city, that beautiful city,
   Music is born and 'tis perfected there;
Voices and harps, the full choir of the ransomed,
   Every sweet melody filling the air.
        The mansions are ringing,
        So grand is the singing,
Never a discord, all harmony there;
        May God's love far-reaching,
        And His Spirit's teaching,
For a home in that city His people prepare.

A WATER-LILY.

Lily white, heart aglow,
   In thy still pond
Blooming in virgin snow,
   No care nor bond,
Roots down in depths below,
   Blossoms beyond.

Where, lily, was thy birth?
   Fragrant and white,
Struggling from miry earth
   Up, up to light,
Thou flower of matchless worth,
   Beautiful, bright.

AMBITION.

I LONGED to act some worthy part
    Or do some noble deed,
Labour that would deserve and win
    Earth's fairest flowers and meed;
Some gift brought to my fellow-men
    Of life, or art, or creed.

I wished, but He who plans for us
    Just bade me work and wait,
Rejoice or suffer humbly here,
    In His own chosen state;
To do my duty every day,
    Unknown to fame or fate.

And He who toiled in Nazareth
    Within the cottage door,
Will own the lowly service done,
    Henceforth, for evermore;
And satisfy each child of His
    From His abundant store.

VICTORIA REGINA.

A GIRLISH form in virgin white,
   With fair hair falling round her face,
Was called at dawn to solemn words,
   " Victoria, Queen, by heaven's grace ! "
The maiden, kneeling at God's throne,
Besought His blessing on her own.

Long years have come and gone since then,
   Tumult of war and song of peace ;
Culture, and art, and wealth have caused
   The white man's growth, the black's release ;
While goodness, industry, and right
Have flourished in the crown's pure light.

When once, like Sheba's Queen of old,
   Men to her land came seeking fame,
She pointed not to throne secure,
   Nations subdued, or honoured name ;
But, "Tell your Prince in 'The Book' lies
The secret of Great Britain's rise."

Golden and Diamond Jubilee
   Have celebrated her long reign
Of righteousness, powerful and wise—
   The sun ne'er sets on her domain ;
Her people's praise is justly loud,
Of Queen and Flag and Country proud.

Empress of India's burning soil,
   Queen of Great Britain and the Isles,
Our virgin "Lady of the Snow"
   Blooms 'neath her gracious sovereign's smiles.
God bless our Queen, we love her yet!
True British hearts will not forget.

That reign, begun in humble prayer,
   In the fresh morn of early days,
Has passed from noon to vesper song;
   Yet brighter glow the sunset rays,
Dispersing far the shades of night;
"At even time it shall be light."

HAPPINESS.

I sought for Pleasure all the hours,
   And everywhere I missed her;
I could not grasp her golden flowers,
   I then turned to her sister
Plain Duty—living not for one,
   I sought for others' pleasure,
When lo, I found that I had won
   True happiness and treasure!

A JUBILEE PRAYER.

JEHOVAH, ruler Thou of earth and heaven,
    The Lord of lords, the everlasting King,
This year of Jubilee, our adoration
    And praise for mercies past to Thee we bring!

We thank Thee for our loved and honoured sovereign,
    And for her world-wide, long, and righteous sway;
For Thou, through her, hast given freedom, plenty,
    The peace that rules throughout our land to-day.

From the rich, verdant shores of dear old England
    Ring out the bells for her triumphant reign;
The Emerald Isle and Scotland's rugged hill-tops
    Re-echo o'er the waves the joyful strain.

The music swells from many a distant island,
    From India's sunny shores beyond the seas,
And from fair Canada and northern regions,
    Where ice and snow enshroud the forest trees.

For many nations throng to do her honour;
    Her upright life has influenced the world;
And peace, and truth, and purity are fruitful
    Wherever Britain's standard is unfurled.

A JUBILEE PRAYER.

But stronger far than all a nation's bulwarks,
    Weapons of war, or statesmen's loyal care,
Is the true homage of a loving people
    Who circle and protect their Queen with prayer.

For hers has been the noblest exaltation,
    The righteousness that lifts a kingdom high;
Thy truth her stronghold and the throne's foundation;
    The record of true greatness cannot die.

Lord, make her reign yet brighter and more glorious,
    Free from all error, famine, bloodshed, loss;
Her sword in future, as of yore, Thy Gospel;
    Her flag the blood-stained banner of the Cross.

Spare her to home and loyal hearts that honour,
    As few have been revered in her estate,
And make the sunset season glowing, peaceful,
    The evening shadows gently falling late.

And when the messenger who comes to all men
    Shall summon her to Thy fair land of light,
May she receive a crown that never fadeth,
    A lasting sceptre and a palace bright.

Forever dwell with those long gone before her,
    And reign with them through an eternal day;
For earthly thrones and titles are but fleeting,
    But heaven's honours never shall decay.

WOMAN.

"God made woman, not from man's head to rule over him, nor from his feet to be trampled on by him, but from his side, under the arm to be protected, and near the heart to be loved."—MATTHEW HENRY.

IN days of yore, long years before
    The world was peopled over,
God's mighty tone made man alone,
    Earth's earliest human lover.

His home was fair—no sin, no care,
    No toil that was not pleasure;
But there apart, the loving heart
    Had none to share its treasure.

Jehovah said that man should wed
    A bride for him created,
And so one night his Eve all bright
    To Adam's soul was mated.

No more alone, "bone of his bone,"
    "Flesh of his flesh," rich finding,
In joy or pain no longer twain,
    One heart two bodies binding.

Not from man's head was his wife led—
    The woman is not master;
Nor from his feet—it is not meet
    That he beneath should cast her.

Below the arm to shield from harm,
    Such is man's bounden duty;
And from his side that he might hide
    Within his heart her beauty.

A creature good of human blood,
    By God Almighty given;
Two side by side can breast life's tide,
    When one alone were riven.

Not raised above, but crowned with love,
    Her home her throne and palace;
Cheerful and kind, with well-trained mind
    That drinks at wisdom's chalice.

Though through her sin once entered in
    To curse and blight the Garden,
Yet through her pain life came again,
    A Saviour's love to pardon.

From heathen night the Gospel light
    The bonds of old is shaking,
But let not pride now turn the tide,
    God's own true order breaking.

Oh, woman meek, haste not to seek
   Those things that are withholden!
But gladly claim thy precious name,
   And nobler deeds embolden.

Thou hast a sphere, thou needst not fear
   That bygone chains will fetter;
But keep thy place, thy woman's grace,
   And man will love thee better.

OLD SONGS, OLD FLOWERS.

The old songs are the sweetest,
   The songs of long ago,
That echoed in the gloaming
   In tender tones and low.
The new songs may be better,
   With greater wisdom glow,
But the old songs are the sweetest,
   The songs of long ago.

The old flowers are the sweetest,
   Their bloom we'll ne'er forget;
The old time garden favourites,
   Sometimes we see them yet.
Skill may produce great marvels,
   And fairer beauties show,
But the old flowers are the sweetest,
   The flowers of long ago.

MY FORTUNE.

Better by far than a lofty position,
   Beauty, or station, or knowledge, or fame,
Silver or gold, or a favoured condition,
   A circle of friends, or a world-honoured name;
Dearer to me than all earth's gifts and pleasures,
   The gems of the land, or the pearls of the sea,
Is the one loving heart with the wealth of its treasures
   Henceforth and forever surrendered to me.

BEAUTY.

We care not whether the friends we prize
   Have beautiful faces or no;
We never consider their looks at all,
   Because we love them so;
We are glad to have them enter our homes,
   And sorry to see them go.

For beauty will come, and beauty will fade,
   And homage is all her due,
But we value a man for his sterling worth,
   Be he old friend or new;
And beautiful faces are those that show
   A heart that is kind and true.

CHARITY.

I Corinthians XIII.

Charity suffereth long,
  And charity envieth not;
Charity is not proud
  Of talent, or wealth, or lot.
Charity does not seek
  Her own sweet self to please;
Charity's kind and meek
  Is spent for others' ease.
Charity will not help
  To slander another's name;
Charity hopes, believes,
  Endures through good or shame.
Charity never fails—
  She comes from heaven above;
Let us copy more of her grace,
  God's wonderful gift of love.

FRIENDSHIP.

Would you know if your friends be many,
   Or if they are tried and true?
How much your admirers, if any,
   Would be willing to do for you?

Just lose your position or money,
   To sickness surrender your health,
Then the bees that fly after your honey
   Will vanish as fast as your wealth.

But the friends who are worthy of knowing
   The closer around you will press;
Affliction their full value showing,
   Sterling gold is their love to possess.

THE CHRISTIAN'S BELIEF.

I believe in God the Father
   Who hath made and loves us all;
I believe in God the Saviour
   Who redeemed us from the fall;
I believe in God the Spirit;
   Who will guide us on our way;
I believe there is a heaven
   We shall enter in some day.

THE PAST.

"Let the dead past bury its dead."—LONGFELLOW.

"LET the dead past bury its dead"
  Where they cannot arise again,
And weary not life, and heart, and head,
  With recalling its ghosts in pain.
For the past has gone forever;
  Then bury it, bury it deep;
From the living its memory sever,
  Let the past its own graves keep.

The present can offer thee treasures
  Of life, and joy, and love,
Happiness, wealth and pleasures,
  Hopes for earth and above.
Then act in the present, living
  For now and the future alone;
And life shall grow rich in giving,
  And heaven shall be thine own.

TIME.

TIME.

"God Himself cannot give us back our lost opportunities."
—Edna Lyall.

A second gone, a minute gone,
   Such a little thing;
An hour gone, a day gone,
   Time is on the wing;
A week gone, a month gone,
   Time flies on apace;
A year gone, a year gone,
   All one year of grace.
Gone now, forever flown
   Far beyond recall;
God Himself can't give it back,
   I have lost it all.

Swift pass the days away
   Like a silver chime;
Thou art growing very gray,
   Old Father Time!
Oh, may I learn thy worth
   And a miser be!
Though the years belong to God,
   The hours belong to me.

A WORD.

A word, and a heart is broken ;
   A word, and we weep in pain ;
A word, and a thought is woken
   That never shall sleep again.

A word, and a strain of singing
   As a beautiful hymn has come ;
A word, and a smart is stinging ;
   A word, and our joy is dumb.

A word, and the faith we cherished
   In another is lying killed ;
A word, and our hope has perished ;
   A word, and our love is stilled.

A word—it is such a trifle
   We scarcely reckon its worth ;
And yet it has power to rifle
   The holiest pleasures of earth.

Let our words be loving and tender,
   Helpful and true each day ;
Some time an account we must render
   Of every word we say.

THE POET.

He chose a little library,
  The cosiest of nooks;
He bought a chair and table,
  And shelves of handsome books.

A desk and pens and paper,
  A silver inkstand bright,
Blotter and knife and pencil,
  Then he sat him down to write.

But the page lay blank before him
  In spite of all his pains,
For in furnishing his study
  He had forgotten brains.

CANADA.

The shores of Old England are precious to me,
Oft in memory's vision her beauties I see;
The mountains of Wales, the fresh Emerald Isle,
And Scotland's rough hill-tops and heathery smile.

The brightness of France will the stranger allure;
The skies of sweet Italy ever are pure;
The Swiss and their Alps still eternally stand;
The Germans aye worship their own fatherland.

Antiquity marvels on China's old shore,
While Egypt's fair ruins lie buried in lore;
In India jungles, Siberia snow,
In Africa deserts and tropical glow.

In Norway and Sweden fresh beauties there be,
And nature's pure life on the isles of the sea;
America, sister, has treasures untold,
Perfection of climate, and life new and old.

Famed, lovely, or ancient historical ground,
In each and in all there is wealth to be found;
But Canada, Canada, land of the free,
From all earth's fair countries my heart turns to thee.

Thy towns and thy cities, thy pleasures, thy gold,
Where intelligence labours for treasures untold !
Where integrity's virtues with industry shine,
And the Beaver and Maple their emblems combine !

Thy forests, thy mountains, thy far-stretching plains,
Where in solitude whistles the north wind its strains;
Ice lands that ne'er melt with the sun's warming breath,
Where the frost-king wraps all in the silence of death.

Thy grandeur, thy vastness, thy richness of store,
Thy lakes and thy fountains flow on evermore;
Thy cataracts mighty unceasingly toll,
Thy rivers untiring in majesty roll.

Thy orchards, thy vintage, thy ripe golden grain,
Thy summer breeze whispering a lover's refrain;
Thy autumn's rich clothing, thy green and thy glow,
Thy winter, thy sleigh-bells, thy glittering snow.

The joys of some nations our country may lack,
Yet give me this land of the old Union Jack;
For dearest by far of the best lands of earth
Is Canada, Canada, home of my birth !

RETROSPECT.

In the trials of age when our warfares wage
    The conflicts of error and truth,
'Tis then are prized what we once despised,
    The burdenless days of youth.

We are growing old; in the shining gold
    Is scattered the silver tress;
We vainly sigh for the youth gone by,
    As its memories fondly press.

For who is there in this world of care
    Who would not be young again?
With strength and life, the short-lived strife,
    The rapturous bliss and bane?

But though older years may bring us tears,
    They carry us gifts as well;
Far deeper pain, but richer the gain,
    And the joys no tongue can tell.

Though charms may fade and Time cast his shade
    On the faces no longer fair,
His lessons meet can leave traces sweet
    That record no waste years there.

More precious store than in days of yore,
    After all we would not choose,
For love grows strong when it waiteth long,
    And we gain if we also lose.

DEATH.

WILL it be suddenly death's hand shall smite—
One moment a shadow, the next the full light—
Eyes closing on earth's scenes to open above
In radiance of glory, perfection of love?

Will he come gradually, silently, cold,
Slow, gentle fingers unloosing earth's hold,
In the night watches repeating his call
To part with these treasures and gain heaven's all?

He is but a messenger sent in his day
The child to the palace of joy to convey;
Then dread not his coming, thou heir to a throne,
For he will but usher thee into thine own.

Ah! then, what matters it how he doth come,
So long as he opens the door into home?
At morning or evening, at midnight or noon,
His coming is never too late or too soon.

"WHO LOVÉD ME."

GALATIANS ii. 20.

"Who lovéd me"—oh, wondrous fact,
   Beyond the ken of mortal man!
Earth's intellect too weak to grasp
   The measure of the Godhead's plan.
Height, depth, length, breadth, I cannot tell,
But that He loves my heart knows well.

"Who lovéd me"—love so divine!
   Eternity alone can trace
The hour in which He first began
   To give me in His heart a place;
The birth and date of love unknown,
But that He loves His Word has shown.

"Who lovéd me"—I cannot say
   Why He loved me so long ago;
E'en earth's foundations were not laid
   When He declares He loved me so.
He planned that I might be His own,
A partner of His name and throne.

"Who lovéd me"—a love that knows
   No fluctuation and no end;

"WHO LOVÉD ME."

To-day as yesterday the same,
   Yea ever, an unchanging Friend.
I cannot tell why I'm so blest,
But He loves me and this is rest.

"Who lovéd me." What shall I do
   For gratitude? What offering give?
My love is all the gift He craves,
   That I should henceforth for Him live,
And to the world around me prove
The fulness of redeeming love.

"Who lovéd me." Then I should love,
   'Tis of discipleship the proof;
From those whom Jesus Christ can love,
   What right has man to stand aloof?
Then teach us ever to proclaim
The love Thou hast to all the same.

And when eternity shall dawn,
   These words shall be our song to Thee:
"Who loved and cleansed us by His blood,
   From condemnation set us free."
Eternity alone can show
The reason why God loved us so.

TO-DAY.

*"Out of eternity the new day is born,
Into eternity at night we return."*
—CARLYLE.

OUT of slumber awaking
  Look upward and say,
"From eternity's breaking
  Another new day."
And as the light's dawning
  Just pray to-day's prayers,
Then bright as the morning
  Go meet to-day's cares.
Enjoy to-day's pleasure,
  Increase to-day's gain,
Gather up to-day's treasure,
  And bear to-day's pain.
Weep for to-day's sorrows,
  Smile at to-day's rest,
To God leave thy morrows,
  With Him they are best.
E'er seeking refreshing,
  Go humbly and pray,
Crave pardon and blessing,
  Give thanks for to-day.
Fear nothing, but rather
  Ask God watch to keep,
And trusting thy Father
  Sink sweetly to sleep.

"GLORIA IN EXCELSIS DEO."

"Glory to God in the highest,
  And peace and good-will on the earth,"
Forgiveness and worship and singing,
  And bringing of presents, and mirth.

Then chant it again, angels holy,
  Earth's glory thus heaven's brief loss,
For the high has come down to the lowly,
  Surrendered a crown for a cross.

Then hasten and worship the Saviour,
  And offer Him gifts of true worth,
Sing "Glory to God in the highest,
  And peace and good-will on the earth."

"TILL THE DAY BREAK."

Smiles and tears, calm and fears,
    Come alike to all on earth;
Peace and pain, bliss and bane,
    Broken heart and happy mirth.
Grief and pleasure, loss and treasure,
    Fairest blossoms, blight, decay;
Change marks all things "till the day break
    And the shadows flee away."

Parting, meeting, laughing, greeting,
    Is the order of the strife;
Love or sorrow come to-morrow;
    None can read the scroll of life.
Resting, working, slaving, shirking,
    Young and aged, 'neath the sun—
Some are sleeping, some are weeping,
    Some with riches, some with none.

Joys and cares, moans and prayers,
    Portioned out to each a share;
Some revealed, some concealed,
    Each soul must a burden bear.
Faith and reason hail the season
    For the breaking of the day,
When in God's own light supernal
    All "the shadows flee away."

REST.

"Rest is not quitting a busy career,
  Rest is just fitting oneself to one's sphere."

Rest is not in longing for some other place,
Wanting others' talents, chances, honours, grace;
Dreaming, idly dreaming, weary of the strife,
Discontented ever with our sphere in life.

Rest is not in seeking for a higher plane,
Wealth and ease and pleasure, joy and love to gain;
Rest is just the doing, with a cheerful grace,
Duties God has given in our appointed place.

"LOVE NEVER FAILETH."

Though dim be now the sparkling eyes
  That used to glance and glow,
The voice grown weak, unmusical,
  The airy footsteps slow;
The locks once bright, abundant,
  Be white with years or care;
The bloom of youth all faded,
  The form no longer fair;
To me thou still art beautiful,
  Love's eyes no difference see;
Though all thy charms have vanished,
  Thou art as dear to me.

WISHES.

"If I were only a woman now"—
   And the tiny maiden sighed,
While dreams of the future furrowed her brow,
   As her fancy wandered wide;
Her pleasures and toys neglecting,
   Unheeding her childhood's boon,
Life's older wisdom rejecting,
   Longed for days that come all too soon.

"If I were only a child again"
   Is the woman's sorrowful wish;
A light heart free from all care and pain,
   A simple and daily bliss.
'Tis true with the toil comes treasure,
   And flowers bloom oft in the way,
But the season of unalloyed pleasure
   Is in childhood's innocent day."

MY BELOVED.

Thou lovest me, oh, wondrous bliss !
Far, far beyond my heart's desire,
My highest wish !
And at thy side my soul is satisfied.
    My all in all thou art;
    Pressed to thine heart
    I feel no care, no fear
    If thou art near.
The consummation of all bliss is this,
To know that thou art mine and I am thine !

I know no other will, no power but thine—
    A slave to thee,
    Yet I am free.
Oh, wondrous liberty of love !
One will all other wills above,
    One at whose feet
    'Tis worship meet
    To bow in adoration sweet,
Offering myself, my heart, my all
In glad surrender to love's call;
No longer desolate to roam,
Within thy bosom is my home,

"DO NOBLE DEEDS, NOT DREAM THEM ALL DAY LONG."

We long for a nobler life that would to others preach,
        And while we sigh
        There lieth by
The things that we all can reach.

We think a kindly thought, but its echo is never heard,
        And the empty parts
        Of lonely hearts
Are missing the loving word.

The acts we mean to perform are lofty, and grand, and true,
        But the minutes fly,
        And the chance slips by
For the good deed we might do.

We hope some fame to win by thought, or deed, or speech,
        And very near
        In our own small sphere,
Great lessons we may teach.

We pray for skilful hands that some good work may be wrought,
        And the gentle touch
        That means so much
Lives only in our thought.

"DO NOBLE DEEDS."

We think of the gladsome work, and praise the willing feet
      Of those who stand
      In the heathen land
And tell the story sweet.

We look for a call to come, direct from glory given,
      While on our street,
      At our very feet,
Are souls we may help to heaven.

We seek for chances great, some mighty act to do,
      And visions that rise
      Obscure from our eyes
The things that lie right in view.

We talk of the future joys, of the crown that may be won,
      And all our way
      Is shadowed to-day
With the things we have left undone.

"WHY STAND YE HERE ALL THE DAY IDLE?"

"Why stand ye here all the day idle?"
    When labourers are scattered and few;
The fields are all whitening to harvest,
    There is work for the weakest to do.
There is ploughing and hedging and ditching,
    And sowing the life-giving seeds;
There is watering and shading and tending,
    And carefully plucking out weeds.
There is watching and training and guarding
    From enemies, cold, and from heat;
There is reaping and binding and garnering,
    The harvesting home of the wheat.
Then stand ye not all the day idle,
    Or your life you will bitterly rue:
This world is in need of your service,
    There is work for each labourer to do.

LITTLE THINGS.

"Little things on little wings lift little souls to heaven."

Only a kindly word
   Lovingly spoken,
In a hard, lonely heart
   Joy is awoken.

Only a helping hand
   Cheerfully given,
One spirit crushed to earth
   Lifts eyes to heaven.

Only a penny small,
   Gratitude's token,
In a far heathen land
   Life's Bread is broken.

Every day's tiny gifts
   Scarce worth the giving,
Yet 'tis the little things
   Make up our living.

And in the better land,
   Whither we're going,
Rich harvest shall be reaped
   After earth's sowing.

ADVICE.

The good advice that we do not want
    We are ready to give away;
We will gladly and cheerfully pass it round
    To rich or poor or gay;
They shall have all that we have on hand,
    And nothing at all to pay.

'Tis the only good in this world of ours
    That is costless, easily found;
In all varieties, every form,
    It doth everywhere abound;
We generously give and bequeath to all,
    We scatter it freely round.

UNSATISFIED.

"Heaven sends almonds to those who have no teeth."
—Spanish Proverb.

On hearts that are closed and barred
   Is poured out a wealth of love,
While those who could show an answering glow
   Must seek for affection above.

The poor and the sick must weep,
   Forsaken by all in their cot,
While the mansion is bright with the friends and the light,
   And companions are needed not.

A man has surrendered his youth,
   To gather up wealth he has toiled,
But sorrow or pain have attended his gain,
   His fortune by suffering is spoiled.

The child who slaves and who pines
   For a kiss or a parent's call,
Must early and late stand aside and wait
   For the child who abandons them all.

AFTERWARDS.

When fortune upon men has smiled
    With pleasure, with ease, or with wealth,
She cometh some day and she taketh away
    The peace, or the friends, or the health.

So things come appointed to all,
    Gold, poverty, suffering, or worth;
There's thus compensation to men of each nation,
    And justice is ruling the earth.

AFTERWARDS.

When we look back, at our journey's end,
    On the way we have travelled o'er,
We will offer thanks to our Heavenly Friend
    For His leading in days of yore.

The sorrow, the joy, the pain, the gloom,
    We will read in eternal light;
The gain, the loss, the despair, the tomb,
    Will glisten with radiance bright.

For now is the school and training days,
    And we follow by faith, not sight;
But afterwards we will sing His praise
    Who hath guided us always right.

COMPENSATION.

The spirit soars highest and longest
    That quivers the most 'neath the cross;
The heart whose affection is strongest
    Has darkest forebodings of loss.
Pain lies near the margin of blessing,
    And smiles are akin to the tears;
The deeper the joy of possessing,
    The greater the doubts and the fears.
Those who suffer the keenest in weeping
    Are quickest the pleasures to see,
And those who know nothing of keeping
    From terror of losing are free.

"LOVE BEGETS LOVE."

Love, and you will be loved;
    Loved, then you too shall love;
Love make the whole world kin,
    And links to worlds above.
'Tis love, pure love, this old earth needs,
    Self-sacrifice and noble deeds—
Not sermons, prayers, and empty creeds,
    But love to God and man.

A FUNERAL.

On earth the bitter sound of voices weeping,
    Pain, or despair, or pity;
In heaven the white-robed holy throng is sweeping
    In glory through the city.

In perfumed darkness here we see the mourning,
    The funeral pall and sorrow;
While there another life is e'en now dawning,
    A new and bright to-morrow.

Here muffled peal of bells from out the steeple
    The last sad message ringing;
There sound the harps of all the ransomed people,
    Angels sweet welcome singing.

Then say not here that those we love are ending
    The life that fain we'd cherish;
They are but gone from us to God's befriending,
    To joys that never perish.

Christ wept. This truth amid our tears we ponder,
    The closer to Him pressing;
They are but taken to His mansion yonder,
    His nearer presence blessing.

For we are but one family, now divided
  By Jordan's narrow portal;
And in the home our Father has provided
  We'll meet in bliss immortal.

EASTER SUNDAY.

Far down the ages ringing
  We hear the silver chime
Of million voices singing,
  This happy Easter time.
Earth music blends with heaven
  To crown our Jesus King,
All power to Him is given,
  All praise to Him we bring.
Oh, grand the wondrous story!
  It was for us He died,
That golden gates of glory
  For us might open wide.
He rose and lives forever
  From death to set us free,
Naught from His love shall sever
  Through all eternity.
Then with one voice upraising
  Let earth her tribute pay,
Our glorious Captain praising
  This resurrection day.

"GO YE INTO ALL THE WORLD AND PREACH THE GOSPEL."

From over the ocean the message
   Is sounded toward you to-day,
From those who in sin have been sleeping;
   " Come over and help us, we pray.
We know not the truth as in Jesus,
   Our nations are lying in night;
Oh, will ye not bring us the gospel,
   Ye people who walk in the light?'

Close, close to your doors comes the story
   Of China's vast millions of souls,
While warm with the breath of the desert
   The message from Africa rolls.
From Siam, Japan, and Corea,
   From India's women in woe,
From lips that are touched with the sunbeams,
   From hearts that are chilled with the snow.

In many a green flowering island,
   Resplendent in nature's array,
In many a country and city,
   A welcome is waiting to-day.
So many are willing to follow
   If some will but show them the light;
But laborers are scanty in number,
   And fields with the harvest are white.

"GO YE INTO ALL THE WORLD."

So many are living and dying
   Who never have heard of the light;
Their lives by the story unsweetened,
   Their death is eternity's night.
While ye to your bosoms are folding
   The book with the Saviour's command,
"Go therefore and teach every creature,
   Proclaiming My word through the land."

Go forward and give them the tidings,
   The wonderful tidings of truth;
They're suited for every condition,
   For childhood, and manhood, and youth.
Then will ye not give them the gospel,
   Ye people that dwell in the light?
Why leave them to stumble in darkness,
   Who might with God's glory be bright?

Then haste ye, arise and be doing,
   Oh, let not the moments be lost;
The Master's "well done," and His praises
   Will more than repay all the cost.
When out of all climes shall be gathered
   A people prepared for the King,
Who in glory and beauty forever
   The praise of Jehovah shall sing.

"WITHOUT SHEDDING OF BLOOD IS NO REMISSION."

HEBREWS ix. 22.

In Christ, who died for me,
Is found my only plea
Before a righteous God.
Without redeeming grace
I cannot, dare not, face
The sins that cost "the Lamb of God" His blood.

In God's most holy sight
It is not might or right
That can for guilt atone.
'Tis not a spotless life,
Nor victory in earth's strife,
But Jesus Christ who saves, and He alone.

All equal, side by side,
No place for human pride
At Calvary's sacred cross.
At those once piercéd feet
The rich and lowly meet,
Earth's rank grows paltry, and its gold but dross.

In Christ's blood, given so free,
Is found my only plea
That He my sins will hide.
He died for me in love,
He rose and reigns above,
And by His life my soul is justified.

"THY WILL BE DONE."

'Tis easy to obey God's voice
When He calls us to rejoice;
But can we, with hearts still tender,
Come to Him in glad surrender
When He bids us work or tarry
In a way we do not choose?
Do we then His will refuse?
Nay, let us more firmly stand
On His love, and place our hand
Closer yet within His own,
Let Him lead, and follow on;
God is good and light will dawn,
For the hearts that draw the nearest
Will the truth the soonest see
That God is a loving Father,
Who would have His children be
Happier than this world can make them,
Peaceful that it cannot shake them,
If they rest on Him alone;
Ever in His grace abiding,
In His promises confiding,
In His sanctuary hiding,
We shall say, "Thy will be done!"
Freely, not from fears compelling,
But because our heart is swelling
With a theme beyond our telling;
God loves us and we love Him.
Faith can pray, "Thy will be done!"
Love whispers low, "Our will is one."

"REST IN THE LORD."

PSALM xxxvii. 7.

"Rest in the Lord," wait patiently,
   Though in love He may long delay;
The light shall shine in that heart of thine,
   And the shadows all flee away.
Though weary and dark and chill the night,
   The morning dawn shall break,
And God's own light make all things bright,
   Thy voice to new songs awake.

"Rest in the Lord," and He shall give
   All that thine heart desires;
In Him be strong, though the time be long,
   And thy weak faith often tires.
All worlds and nations are in His hands,
   And shall He not care for thee?
Trust and be still, till He shows His will,
   Then follow, whate'er it be.

"Rest in the Lord," His tender heart
   Loves better than earth's best love;
Our hearts fain lean on the loved ones seen,
   And forget the great heart above.

"REST IN THE LORD."

He seeks to be first, yield all to Him,
  On the sure foundation rest;
Love cannot grow dim with its source in Him,
  Then earth shall be truly blest.

"Rest in the Lord," wait His good time,
  Calm all thy foreboding fears;
Cloud not the ray of the present day
  With the shadow of coming years.
He surely can lead through all the path,
  Who hath brought thee safe thus far;
See, above the strife of thy daily life
  Gleams the light of Hope's guiding star.

"Rest in the Lord," whate'er thy way,
  Whatever thy trouble be;
Hast thou not heard in His own dear Word
  How His heart doth rest in thee?
The saints are the King's inheritance,
  Then fear not, He cares for thee;
He will lead aright to the land of light,
  Thou His joy and crown shall be.

THANKSGIVING DAY.

Here we raise our Ebenezer
    For the blessings of the year—
Peace and plenty, fruit and vintage,
    Rain and snow, and sun and cheer,
Land protected, life extended,
    Seedtime, summer, harvest, sure—
Once again we prove God's promise,
    Know His mercies still endure.

Seeds dropped in the earth in darkness,
    Scattered broadcast o'er the field,
Grown apace to golden beauty,
    An abundant harvest yield.
Faith and then the full fruition,
    Though the waiting time seemed long;
Now we raise our Ebenezer,
    Harvest home and reapers' song.

Deepest thanks we fain would offer
    For our highly favoured land,
And a year's continued comforts,
    Blessings countless as the sand.
Praise of lips and adoration,
    Heartfelt love and homage bring;
Here we raise our Ebenezer,
    As the Harvest Home we sing.

THE APOSTLES' CREED.

I BELIEVE in God the Father,
    The Almighty King of kings,
Eternal and invisible,
    Who made and loves all things.
I believe in God the Saviour,
    Born as Mary's lowly child,
Who suffered under Pilate,
    Yet was loving, meek, and mild;
Was crucified, and buried
    In Hades' deepest gloom,
Has risen and ascended
    As victor o'er the tomb.
I believe that He is coming
    As our triumphant Head,
The Lord of all the universe,
    To judge the quick and dead.
I believe in God the Spirit,
    Sent to lead us on the road;
Who maketh intercession
    In His divine abode.
I believe in a church united,
    A fellowship of soul;
I believe in sins forgiven,
    Salvation that makes whole.
And I believe our bodies
    Shall rise and live again
In glory everlasting,
    A life that knows no pain.

NOTHING.

"For we brought nothing into this world, and it is certain we can carry nothing out."—1 TIMOTHY vi. 7.

WE came to the world with nothing,
And with nothing we must return;
    Then let not the greed
    Of earth's selfish creed
The spirit's best qualities spurn.

We came to the world with nothing,
And we nothing can take away;
    The work of our hands,
    Our possessions and lands,
All our silver and gold, must stay.

We came to the world with nothing,
We go, and we know not when;
    No friend or lover,
    The whole world over,
Can be a companion then.

We came to the world with nothing,
And we nothing can take away
    But a hope in the Lord,
    And a faith in His word,
And a spirit that liveth for aye,

"THE LORD IS MY SHEPHERD."

Psalm XXIII.

The God everlasting, the mighty Jehovah,
   Creator of heaven, of sea, and of land,
This Lord is "my Shepherd," I never can perish,
   He holdeth the sheep of His flock in His hand.

"The Lord is my Shepherd," no want can alarm me,
   He guideth his sheep to the tenderest food;
He maketh them rest by the side of "still waters,"
   Withholding no blessing that is for their good.

He healeth, restoreth, and leadeth His chosen
   In pathways of righteousness day after day;
In the "valley of shadow" I fear not the evil,
   "His rod" and "His staff" will give comfort and stay.

"The Lord is my Shepherd," no foes can o'erthrow me,
   He provideth, anointeth, and filleth with joy;
His "goodness and mercy" shall follow me ever,
   The peace that He giveth none else can destroy.

"The Lord is my Shepherd," and I shall dwell with Him
   Forever and ever in glory untold,
When as the "Chief Shepherd" He cometh to gather
   The far scattered sheep of His flock in one fold.

TRUTH.

JOHN xviii. 38; xiv. 6; xvii. 17.

"WHAT is truth?" This solemn question
   Cometh from the lips of all,
Echo of that scene enacted
   Once in Pilate's judgment hall,
When before the earthly ruler
   Stood the Christ, the King of all,
Humbly, lonely, as a felon
   Waiting for the law to fall.

"What is truth?" It is not knowledge,
   Born of earth and fed by man,
For the world's best education
   May be built on error's plan;
And the system now victorious,
   Winning men's sincerest trust,
May prove fallible to-morrow,
   And be crumbling in the dust.

"What is truth?" It is not doctrine,
   'Tis not preacher, church, or creed;
Teachers now are so divided
   None could say which meets his need.

Preachers, critics, and professors,
   Gray-haired age and beardless youth,
All are eager in discussion,
   Finding fault, rejecting truth.

"What is truth?" Hush, hear the answer,
   Jesus speaks: "'I am the Truth,'
From the everlasting ages
   On to heaven's eternal youth.
I am Truth, why seek for error
   When the Truth thine own may be?
Do not starve on disquisitions
   When the 'Bread of Life' is free."

"What is truth?" Again 'tis answered
   By the pen of grace divine,
Hark! "Thy Word is truth." Then, brethren,
   Seek not truth to undermine.
God is truth, and truth must conquer,
   Truth is God and will prevail,
Light will surely cast out darkness,
   Error before truth must quail.

Folks may sneer, neglect the Bible,
   Scorn and cavil, laugh or hate;
Men of science may reject it,
   "Higher critics" mutilate,

So-called Christians may defend it,
   Yet refuse the truth it gives;
Man and devil join to crush it,
   Yet forevermore it lives.

Pause then, brethren, truth rejectors,
   'Tis the God of truth you mock;
"Dust to dust" your theories vanish,
   Still immovable the Rock!
Casting off the Truth you perish,
   On the Truth you're saved and stayed;
Truth is infinite, and cannot
   By a finite mind be weighed.

NO ROOM.

"He came unto his own, and his own received him not."
—John i. 11.

No room in the inn
   For the heaven-born stranger,
His home in a stable,
   His cradle a manger.
No room in the palace,
   No room in the cot,
He came to His own
   And they welcomed Him not.

A LEGEND.

The lights burned low in the village streets,
    The inhabitants, wearied, slept;
The toilers rested, all din was hushed,
    And the mourners no longer wept.
The anvil, hammer, and saw were still,
    The day had resigned to night;
E'en the tiny birds in their downy nests
    Were wrapt in a slumber light,
When quietly down through the sleeping town,
    The deserted and silent street,
Came a poor despised wayfaring man
    With weary and painful feet.
He paused at a lock with a gentle knock,
    And petition to let him stay,
But they paid scant heed to his cry of need,
    And flung him a scornful "Nay."
From house to house he went slowly on,
    But each an admission denied;
Some the door locked, and others mocked,
    But by all was his claim defied.
He came at last to a humble home,
    A peasant's poor lowly cot,
But rich was the store within its door,
    A sacred and honoured spot.
They hastened to open, and to him they bring
    The best that the house can afford—

Shelter and comfort, and clothing and food,
   As they would have done unto their Lord.
When suddenly changing, before their rapt eyes
   Stood the Maker of earth and of heaven—
The dwelling was filled with the blessing of God,
   For it was to the Master they'd given.
He thanked them and smiled as He uttered these words
   (While a vision of glory they see),
"Inasmuch as ye did it to one of the least
   Ye have done it indeed unto Me."

PROCRASTINATION.

"NEVER put off till to-morrow
   The thing you can do to-day,"
The opportunity may be gone,
   The desire have passed away.
Live, act, and speak in the present,
   Do noble deeds that shall last,
For the future will gather its shadows
   From neglected work in the past.
The chances which you have wasted,
   The years that have slipped away,
Will gather around to mock you
   In the light of the judgment day.

IF WE HAD KNOWN.

If we had known 'twas the last time
   We and our friend were meeting,
Last chance of hearing counsel wise,
   Or cheerful word of greeting.

If we had known that warm hand clasp
   Would be our last forever,
That Jordan's stream in a few hours
   From earthly life would sever.

If we had known the cheery tone
   By sympathy awoken,
The friendly wish, the kind "good-bye,"
   Last words that we'd hear spoken.

If we had known the flowers we brought,
   The living hand receiving,
Would lie upon the still cold form
   After the spirit's leaving.

Ah, if we knew, how oft we'd add
   To other lives completeness!
And make the hours within our grasp
   Serve memory's future sweetness.

Alas, we may not, cannot know
   Death's mystery perplexing,
But grace can raise all coming days
   Beyond death's power of vexing.

DUTY.

I CANNOT do great things for God
    To make this world the better;
I cannot part one burdened heart
    From care's corroding fetter.
I cannot thrill men's hearts like Paul,
    And make their lives grow sweeter;
I have no call to leave my all
    To follow Christ, like Peter.

I cannot hear His voice on earth,
    Joy from His presence gleaning;
Like John of old His arms enfold,
    While on His bosom leaning.
But if I'm where He places me,
    There is my field of labour;
To God be true, my duty do
    To Him, myself, my neighbour.

He watches o'er each child of His,
    Though poor and prone to stumble;
Each has a place in His great heart,
    However weak or humble.
And this I know He loves me so—
    This truth should make life sweeter;
I am as precious in His eyes
    As Paul, or John, or Peter.

GRAY HAIRS.

Gray hairs, they speak of childhood past,
    Of dreams fulfilled or hopes decayed,
Summer by winter's snows o'ercast,
    Spring merged in autumn's genial shade;
Time's pearly fingers' gentle touch,
    Some riches lost thou gainest much.

The careless happiness of youth,
    The joyous singing time, has flown;
The world and hearts, science and truth,
    And weightier treasures, are thine own;
Freedom to speak, to live, to love,
    As actuated from above.

A crown of gold in days of yore,
    Surmounted by a crown of flowers,
Now "crown of glory," evermore
    Marking the onward fleeting hours;
Then mourn not thus at time's swift flow,
    Blossoms must fade e'er fruit can grow.

THE SPARROW.

Oft out in the rain and the shadow,
   Alone in the snow and the cold ;
Neither beauty, nor wisdom, nor prowess,
   Neither mansion, nor storehouse, nor gold.
In the drought and the heat of the summer,
   In the winter so drear and so long,
I hear a sweet lesson worth learning
   From the little brown sparrow's low song.

Forsaken by all other songsters
   Is our land in its blight and its snow ;
They fly to a shore more congenial
   In beauty of tropical glow.
But the humble brown sparrow stays with us,
   Though buffeted even by man,
And chirps on his note of contentment,
   Still doing the best that he can.

He builds him a nest high and cosy ;
   Man ruins it, right 'neath his face ;
He loses no moment repining,
   Rebuilds in a more secure place.
He has no guarantee for the future,
   Nor knows where his next meal is found ;
He trusts all his care to his Maker,
   And his life shall not fall to the ground.

Shall He who created the sparrows,
   Who giveth all creatures their meat,
Neglect even one of His children
   That dwelleth down here at His feet?
Ah no, He will never forget us!
   His word we may trust and feel strong,
And learn a sweet note of contentment
   From the little brown sparrow's low song.

A BOY.

Two little busy hands,
   Dirty at best;
One little wagging tongue,
   Never at rest;
Two little listening ears,
   Feet seldom still,
Sweet little rosy mouth,
   One sturdy will.
One little trusting heart,
   Two sparkling eyes,
One earnest, childish mind,
   Eager and wise.
One never dying soul
   To mortal given;
One more to grow a man
   Fitted for heaven.

LOVE.

Love is divine; her source is found
In heaven, not earth—'tis holy ground;
She knows no break, no fluctuation,
Is measured not by time's duration.

Love is forgiving, matchless, true,
An old, old story ever new;
Love knows no chains, no limitation,
No sacrifice, and no cessation.

Love is aye kind, she suffereth long;
Love never will her subject wrong;
Love's uncomplaining, gentle, tender,
Companion sweet and leal defender.

Love will all earthly difference sink,
The lightest yet the strongest link;
All else below is fading, altering,
But love is changeless, never faltering.

Love far exceeds all gifts of worth;
Love is God's greatest boon to earth;
Love is eternal, richest treasure,
She knows no birth, no death, no measure.

"HE KNOWETH OUR FRAME."

Psalm ciii. 14.

"He knoweth our frame." He was "made like His brethren,"
    Partakers with them of the same flesh and blood;
The God was made man-like that man might be God-like,
    Joint heir with the Son in the kingdom of God.

"He knoweth our frame." He was homeless, forsaken,
    "Despised and rejected," oft weary and worn;
Hungry and thirsty, more poor than the lowest,
    His cradle a manger, His coronet thorn.

"He knoweth our frame," every fibre and feeling,
    The thoughts that we cannot express if we would;
How we value a friend that can thus comprehend us,
    For the bitterest pain is being misunderstood.

"He knoweth our frame," what a comfort to hear it,
    Though all those about us may not understand;
He knoweth the spirit, the mind, and the body,
    He holdeth the pulse of our life in His hand.

"He knoweth our frame," as the skilful physician
    Reads signs that mean nothing to ignorant eyes,
And knows how to treat us—we rest in that knowledge,
    In confidence taking whate'er he supplies.

Physician Divine, may we trust in Him likewise,
   Receive uncomplainingly what He shall send;
For care is the tenderest coupled with wisdom,
   He is a physician as well as a friend.

"He knoweth our frame," and He never will give us
   A burden too heavy for our strength to bear;
He never forgets or confuses His people,
   He knows each one's frame, and the weakness or care.

He loveth and knoweth, divine and yet human;
   We joy in His love, in His wisdom we trust;
Then let us consider this truth and take courage,
   "He knoweth our frame," He remembers we're dust.

PAIN.

Oh, the mystery of pain!
   Why it comes we cannot tell,
And we shrink beneath its touch
   Though sent by One who loves us well.
Part of earthly training here,
   Discipline in heaven's rule;
We can patient be and learn
   From the Master in His school.

CHRISTMAS MORNING.

Jesus is born! tell the wonderful story,
    Publish it far o'er the lands of the earth;
Angels once brought us the message of glory,
    Singing to herald Messiah's low birth.
Born in a stable and laid in a manger,
    "Made like His brethren," salvation to bring,
That He might rescue His people from danger,
    Save them, and make them the heirs of a King.

Ages have rolled since the light of God's city
    Streamed o'er the shepherds on Bethlehem's plain,
Showing the Father's most marvellous pity,
    In visiting mankind in mercy again;
Sending a Saviour both human and holy,
    Creator and Sovereign as babe to be born;
More precious each year to the saints, high or lowly,
    Is the Jesus who came on that first Christmas morn.

THE WORD.

PSALM xix. 7-13.

The Lord's law is perfect,
   Converting the soul,
Healing the sinner,
   And making him whole.
God's law is so sure
   That the fool it makes wise;
It rejoices the heart,
   And enlightens the eyes.
It is lasting and righteous,
   And true as of old;
It is sweeter than honey
   And richer than gold;
It shelters from danger,
   It cleanses from sin,
And makes a man holy
   Without and within.

SAFETY.

CHRISTIAN barque. sailing on,
    Dread not the blast;
Soon shall the billows rough
    Of earth's sea be past;
Though its tempestuous winds
    Blow over thee,
They do but speed thee on
    Where thou wouldst be.
Winds, waves, and storms unite;
    None can o'erwhelm
A vessel, e'er so frail,
    With Christ at the helm.

Sail on in sun or shade;
    Thy course is straight
From earthly anchorage
    To Zion's gate.
Carry thy flag unfurled,
    Show all thy light;
Others may see the beams,
    Lost in the night.
O'er smooth and smiling seas,
    When storms o'erwhelm,
"Fear not," thy ship is safe—
    Christ's at the helm.

"A LITTLE WHILE."

Sails flying, banner white
   Floats in the breeze,
Thy chain and anchor holds
   In wildest seas;
No storm, howe'er it beats,
   Thy course can check,
And 'tis impossible
   Thy barque to wreck.
Winds, waves, and storms unite;
   None can o'erwhelm
A vessel, e'er so frail,
   If Christ's at the helm.

"A LITTLE WHILE."

"A LITTLE while" as pilgrims here we roam,
"A little while" before the rest of home;
"A little while" of patient, tender care,
"A little while" of faith, and love, and prayer;
"A little while" of earthly joy or sorrow,
"A little while" and hope will dawn to-morrow;
"A little while" of suffering or of loss,
"A little while" to nobly bear the cross;
"A little while," then lay life's duties down;
"A little while" to win the golden crown;
"A little while" of sunshine or of night;
"A little while," then heaven's eternal light.

RICHES.

"Seek not riches but such as thou mayest get justly, use soberly, distribute cheerfully, and leave contentedly."—BACON.

Get no more gold than thou canst gain
    With justice to thy brother;
Cringe not to rich, oppress not poor,
    Nor hurt nor rob another.

Wish no more money in thine hoard
    Than thou canst use with pleasure;
For fear of thieves, of fire, or loss,
    Will spoil the choicest treasure.

Seek not more wealth than thou canst give
    With joy, some others blessing;
To clothe the naked, heal the sick,
    Relieve from wants oppressing.

When sought and won earth's golde chain,
    Let not its fetters bind thee;
Crave no more wealth than thou canst leave
    Without a pang behind thee.

OLD OCEAN.

Have you ever strolled
Where the waters rolled
In fiercely from the ocean,
And heard the swell
Its music tell
Of everlasting motion?

Its pearly foam
On the yellow loam
In playful capers dashing,
Or its billows lock
The mighty rock
With indignation lashing?

Its wavelets dance
On its broad expanse
Beneath the sunbeams' flashes,
Or dark and drear
As it groans in fear
When heaven's thunder crashes?

Into the soul
Its dirges roll,
With life and death 'tis teeming;
Mariners' sail,
And last sad wail,
Its echoes and its dreaming.

      Its waters lave
      O'er many a grave,
The funeral hymn completing.
      From age to age
      Its warfares wage,
Advancing or retreating.

      Though low its beach,
      It cannot reach
Beyond the line appointed;
      Its sand, its shell,
      Its mystic swell,
Are all with speech anointed.

      And so the sea
      Aye talks to me
Of love, and power, and duty;
      Though it is rife
      With death and life,
'Tis harmony and beauty.

SPRING.

The snow has departed, the showers are descending,
  The North's chilling breezes no longer are rife;
The leaves, from their winter seclusion unbending,
  Are kissed by the sun to fresh beauty and life;
The flowers, wrapt in sleep in the earth, are awaking;
  The sweet warblers' music is heard in our land;
The grass her fair emerald garment is taking,
  All nature refashioned by Spring's skilful hand.
The rivers and lakes, free from Winter's cold fingers,
  Flow merrily onward again in their way;
The Frost King's reign ended, while Summer yet lingers,
  Spring comes to foretell and prepare for her sway.

A BIRTHDAY WISH.

May happiness and health and wealth
  Be yours on this and every day;
And love and friends and peace attend
  Each future milestone on your way.
Yours be an overflowing measure,
The best of earth's and heaven's treasure.

SNOW.

The west wind is sighing,
For summer is dying,
Snow hastens here flying
   The winter to bring;
Its touch chill with feeling
New beauty revealing,
And merry bells pealing
   With melody ring.

The clouds are unbending,
Their purity sending,
Their white garment lending
   To cover the earth,
To hide desolation,
And summer's cessation,
A matchless creation
   Proclaims Winter's birth.

No noise, softly falling
In silence appalling,
Old seasons recalling,
   And days that are done.
Its mantle far reaches,
It covers sore breaches,
And charity teaches
   Us "under the sun."

Behold how it flurries,
In ecstasy scurries,
As voiceless it hurries
   On earth to alight.
It is an old story,
With age it is hoary,
Yet ever with glory
   Its coming is bright.

'Tis Santa Claus' weather,
Boreas's feather,
The two live together
   Up near the Northland,
Where the Frost King is dwelling,
His fairies compelling
To flutter here telling
   Us winter's at hand.

TAKE THE SWEET.

Gather up the sunshine lying in your way,
Look upon the bright side every coming day;
Though the storms may lower and the darkness pain,
Watch ye out for God's bow shining after rain.
Though there's thorns and troubles in this world of ours,
Leave the weeds and bitter, take the sweets and flowers.

WINTER.

Gathered sheaves, falling leaves,
    Autumn winds go sighing;
Everywhere, bleak and bare,
    Nature speaks of dying.
Type of death, yet each breath
    Contradiction giving;
Leaves fast falling, past recalling,
    Emblems are of living.

Seedtime, weeping, harvest, reaping,
    Seasons gone forever;
Snow and cold upon the wold,
    Ice upon the river.
Frosty King now can bring
    Blight and malediction
In the room of summer's bloom
    And mild jurisdiction.

Summer flowers from winter hours
    Gather much of sweetness;
Harvest bloom from winter's gloom
    Reaps a rich completeness.
What the cost? What is lost
    When the north winds cover
All the glory with mantle hoary
    Like a white-clad lover?

Sowing, reaping, joy or weeping
   Come in the appointed tide;
Drought, refreshing, bane or blessing,
   Weal or woe are sanctified;
For the living means the giving,
   Graces each the other lends,
And contentment, not resentment,
   Shall work out God's glorious ends.

Upward growing, ever knowing
   Sun will surely follow cloud—
Aye outreaching for the teaching,
   Nature's voices utter loud.
After sorrow dawns a morrow,
   Summer peace for winter strife;
For the giving means the living,
   Death is but the shroud of life.

"SUFFER AND BE STRONG."

'Tis a mighty lesson learned,
   Though it taketh long,
In pain of body, grief of mind,
   Tears or woe or wrong,
Not to worry or repine,
   But "suffer and be strong."

A FABLE.

The Sun and the Wind had a quarrel one day
   As to which of the two was the stronger;
Each persisted in thinking his was the best way,
   And the warfare waxed louder and longer.
At length an old traveller coming along,
   All further disputings they tarried,
And made this the test (who was right and who wrong),
   To unfasten the cloak that he carried.
"You shall have the first chance," said the Sun to the
      Breeze,
   So he rose up and whistled and flurried,
Till he shook all the leaves on the top of the trees,
   But the man only shivered and hurried.
He drew his cloak round him and fastened it tight,
   Right glad that its warmth he was under;
The Wind fiercely blew with his cold and his might,
   Vainly trying to tear it asunder.
Said the Sun to the Wind, as he came for his turn,
   "This cloak from the man I will rifle;"
So he shone till the light of his presence did burn,
   And the garment was opened a trifle.
At length 'twas unfastened, then taken right off,
   The man found it too warm for his pleasure.
Said the Sun to the Wind, "You had better not scoff
   Any more at my power or my treasure."

Dear reader, if you'd have your influence felt,
   This fable of old oft remember—
The sunshine of kindness is surer to melt
   Than the blasts of an angry December.
For "love begets love," and a soft word will break
   The strongest and heaviest fetter;
While coldness will freeze what the sun will awake,
   The kind plan is always the better.

"BE THOU FAITHFUL."

Do THE work that's given to you,
   Whether it be great or small;
He who would be counted worthy
   Must not choose his task at all.

Do the duties that lie nearest,
   Pluck the flowers along the way;
Render prompt and cheerful service,
   Do not waste the present day.

Do not shun the little labours,
   If you would win true renown;
He that's faithful—not successful—
   Shall receive the promised crown.

LINES ON THE DEATH OF A LITTLE GIRL.

She is gone to the land of the blessed,
　Forevermore sheltered from harm
In the Good Shepherd's beautiful pastures,
　Where He carries the lambs in His arm.
By the side of the clear flowing river,
　'Neath the shade of the life-giving tree,
She knows the full worth of the welcome,
　" Let the little ones come unto Me."

She is gone; and though here we may miss her,
　And many a heart tie be riven,
'Tis a link in the chain everlasting
　Connecting our earth-life with heaven.
They die not, those pure and immortal
　Whose feet have crossed over the line;
In beauty and glory resplendent
　In Jesus' own presence they shine.

She is gone, and though sadness is reigning,
　And many the longings and tears,
Be it far from the hearts that so loved her
　To recall to earth's sorrowful years.
The world's highest place is far lower
　Than sitting above at Christ's feet;
Joy there is unsullied with trouble,
　Here bitter is mixed with the sweet.

She is gone, and her home is in shadow,
   Missing childish and innocent glee,
But she is in keeping far better,
   From all sin's defilement now free;
At home, never longer to wander
   O'er deserts so barren and wild,
In the home of her Heavenly Father
   Her own father welcomes his child.

In the school of the greatest of teachers
   She now has been given a place,
Promoted from suffering to glory,
   From faith to the sight of His face.
From life here so brief and unruffled
   To where they shall never grow old,
But in fulness of rapture forever
   Are gathered one flock in one fold.

LIFE'S SEA.

Our Captain and Pilot, we'll ever trust Thee
When storms are raging on life's troubled sea.
In fair or foul weather, whate'er our lot be,
     Stay ever near our side,
     Let us in Thee abide,
     Safe to Thy haven guide,
       Saviour of all.

IN MEMORIAM.

At home, safe home! The angels wake the melody of heaven,
While to the blood-washed ransomed throng another soul is given.
   The gold harps ring,
   The angels sing,
  They tell the same old story;
   And welcome home,
   No more to roam,
  An heir of God and glory.

At home, safe home! With her he loved, forever and forever,
They sit beside the tree of life, they walk beside the river!
   Oh, happy land
   Where God's own hand
  Shall join our lives in one,
   Where heart from heart
   No more shall part,
  And sorrow's days are done!

TO A LITTLE GIRL ON HER FIRST CHRISTMAS.

I wish you a Merry Christmas, this first that you spend on earth,
Sunshine, and health, and treasure, plenty, and peace, and mirth!
May He who in David's city as a little child was born,
Give you blessing that adds no sorrow this happy Christmas morn.

May the best and tenderest music in your ears be daily heard,
Your heart be ever a stranger to the smarting, unkind word;
May you never be wounded, burdened, weary, sad, or alone,
Love and true friends be many, hatred and foes unknown.

May you pluck's earth's fairest blossoms with never a thorn to sting,
Your joys be sweet and lasting, your troubles soon on the wing;
May you little feel of the shadow, and constantly walk in light,
And learn but by others telling the darkness of sorrow's night.

TO A LITTLE GIRL.

May God's hand smooth the pathway that awaits your baby feet,
May you nothing know of earth's bitter, and taste to the full of its sweet;
The unalloyed pleasure of childhood still attend you in later years,
The gifts and the smiles be frequent, and seldom and few the tears.

May Time in his onward marches deal tenderly ever with you,
As you grow "in wisdom and stature," a woman noble and true;
The best, the brightest, the purest, aye uppermost in your life,
Loving and loved and happy as maiden, woman, and wife.

May you early follow the footsteps of Him who this day was born,
Thus each succeeding year will bring a happier Christmas morn;
And when earth's journey is ended, and changes and seasons o'er,
May you find a place in the "Homeland" where they measure by time no more,

LINES TO A YOUNG LADY ON HER WEDDING DAY.

In silk and laces,
Diamonds and graces,
With merry faces
   They crown thee queen.
Oh, happy maiden,
With true love laden,
A woman's Aidenn,
   No serpent seen!

Solemn words spoken,
The golden token,
Vows ne'er be broken
   Throughout thy life.
At the altar kneeling,
The promise sealing,
Then glad bells pealing
   Proclaim thee wife.

The sunlight presses
Thy golden tresses,
Friends with caresses
   Around thee come.
Tears and smiles showing
Sweet roses throwing,
Good wishes glowing,
   No lip is dumb.

ETERNITY.

May thy defender
Prove true and tender,
And bliss engender,
   Aye love and hold.
Sworn one forever,
To part, no never
Till death shall sever
   With fingers cold.

ETERNITY.

Eternity, eternity, thy confines draw e'er near!
We sleep; we know not when our souls again shall waken
   here.
We catch the welcome from thy shore to others gathered
   home,
No longer numbered with the hosts who o'er this country
   roam.

We may not know, we cannot tell, how close or far thou
   art—
Leagues up beyond the shining sun, or near each beating
   heart.
Mystery incomprehensible until we hear the call
That opens up thy portal wide and teaches all in all.

A MODERN SATIRE.

"Whence comes it, dear Mæcenas, that we find
Each to applaud his neighbour's lot inclined?"
—HORACE. Satire I.

"I WISH I was a man," the infant whines
When childish mind at adult will repines.
"Would I were but a child again," man cries,
While bygone pleasures flit before his eyes.
"I would that I were married," sighs the maid,
"A home, sweet children, and a husband staid."
"Were I but single," sobs the o'er burdened wife,
When sinking 'neath the many cares of life.
"If I were but a man," says woman meek,
"I'd do great things and glorious honours seek;
'Tis true man's labour is from sun to sun,
But woman's petty work is never done."
"I'd like to be a woman one brief day,"
So scoffs her lord, "her tasks are but child's play."
Clever musician longs for artist's skill,
Each transient picture to produce at will;
The artist yearns for poet's power to write,
The poet grasps for statesman's seat and might.
The poor man, slaving daily at the soil,
Covets the rich man's ease from earthly toil,
And says, "If I were only rich I'd be
The happiest man alive on land or sea."

"Give me the poor man's peace and rugged health,"
Thus groans the millionaire amid his wealth.
The farmer wishes for a house in town,
The city man for woodland, stream, and down;
The beggar longs as king to win renown—
"Uneasy lies the head that wears the crown."
And so each covets thus the other's grace,
Dissatisfied with their appointed place;
Unheeding gifts that hourly towards them lean,
Forgetting oft to look behind the scene.
"All is not gold that glitters," and the pain
Often outweighs the real or fancied gain.
Then let us be content with our own lot,
And other's gifts or pleasures envy not.

DISCIPLES.

Why stand ye thus gazing, ye saints, into heaven?
    Haste, scatter the news of the Gospel abroad;
Go labour and love, for to you it is given
    To add to the kingdom and joy of your Lord.

Blessed by the Master, and filled with the Spirit,
    Serve Him below through His infinite love;
And in the years to come, saved by His merit,
    Ye shall dwell with Him in glory above.

CUPID.

His far-famed bow I did not know,
　He was to me a stranger;
Coming unsought, I had no thought
　My heart might be in danger.

'Twas closely locked. He came and knocked,
　And threw me in a letter;
His breath I felt, my heart did melt,
　He bound me with his fetter.

He said my heart and I must part,
　He gave it to a stranger;
He laid a claim upon my name,
　My freedom was in danger.

From day to day he won his way,
　By words and looks beguiling;
No more my own, my heart's his throne,
　And there sits Cupid smiling.

His bow was bent, his arrow sent,
　He bound me with his fetter;
But 'twas all gain, I'll not complain,
　He made me richer, better.

True heart and joy without alloy,
　A love that naught can sever;
Though years may fly, Cupid and I
　Are firm, good friends forever.

"THE GREATEST OF THESE IS LOVE."

Faith can grasp the precious promise written in the living Word,
Hope can see the future glories, substance of the things she's heard;
Love can feel the glories **present, Love** can on the promise rest,
Love **can reach** the God of Heaven, lay her head upon His breast.

Faith can make this world a palace, and bring heaven down to earth;
Hope can gild the cloud with silver, and turn sadness into mirth;
Love can only find her dwelling in the heart of Him she loves;
In His arms she proves her heaven, at His voice alone she moves.

Faith and Hope are but as angels who can lead to Zion's land;
Love has entered, and forever holds the key within her hand;
Love will make the sweetest music that shall echo from that shore;
Faith and Hope go back to earth life, Love reigns there forevermore.

CHRISTMAS.

Blest star of the morning, we hail thy bright coming!
   Long years have the nations been waiting this day.
As sunlight dispels all the mists of the dawning,
   So darkness and shadow shall now flee away.

A Saviour is born, a Redeemer is given,
   Awake, earth, and echo the angels' refrain;
The Messiah has come, spread abroad the glad tidings
   O'er mountain and valley, o'er woodland and plain.

Ages have rolled since that first Christmas morning
   When Judah's dark hilltops were gilded with light,
And still 'tis Thy pardon, Thy power, and Thy presence
   That save us and keep us through earth's deepest night.

Born in a stable, the Lord of all glory,
   Suffering and dying salvation to bring;
So we remember Thy first lowly coming,
   And wait for Thy second as conquering King.

FAITH.

Faith is the evidence of things unseen,
   The confidence of all our earthly hope.
Without her we are drifting, wrecked between
   Two worlds—no anchor, sail, or rope
     To help us to the haven we desire.

CHRIST.

Through Christ alone we're saved,
   In Christ for Christ we live;
We learn of Christ to work for Christ,
   Christ all the power must give.
With Christ we dwell below in love,
   And face to face see Christ above.

ONLY.

Only a little word spoken in love,
Only a weary soul pointed above;
Only a kindly act, a tender smile,
Only a burdened heart cheered for awhile.
Only an angry word kept back by prayer,
Only a loving thought cherished with care;
Only a tiny coin cheerfully given,
Only a grateful heart lifted to heaven;
Only a battle fought, a victory won,
Only sin vanquished and the right done;
Only the little things make up the great,
Only work earnestly, time will not wait;
And at the close of life Jesus will say,
"Faithful in little things, now crowned for aye."

"TIME ENOUGH."

"There is plenty of time!" We delay, while confessing
The tasks of the present are many and pressing,
And duties neglected ne'er bring us a blessing.

"There is plenty of time;" so we dally with pleasure,
Assuring ourselves we have plenty of leisure,
And wasting our talents, our time, and our treasure.

"There is plenty of time, we will do it to-morrow,"
The labour of love or the lightening of sorrow,
So a few minutes more from the future we borrow.

"There is plenty of time;" so we dream, while time's
    dying,
And friends are departing and chances are flying,
Sometime to regret with vain sorrow and sighing.

"There is plenty of time!" so we idle, not feeling
The woe that upon us silently stealing,
The bells of eternity even now pealing.

GREATNESS.

At last we learn the truly great
   Are those who walk the ordered way,
Whether it be in public deeds
   Or in the cross of every day.
Humble or high, it matters not,
   For good men are not always great,
And as the poet sweetly saith,
   " They also serve who stand and wait."

We do not seek to choose our lot,
   We scarce would venture if we might,
Our finite minds would surely err,
   What God's appointed must be right.
He sees the smallest, faintest light,
   Though it to earthly eyes looks dim—
The faithful in His sight are great,
   And they shall all be blessed by Him.

HE LEADETH.

When like a thick curtain the cloud of some sorrow
   Obscures from our vision the bright land of rest,
Then, trusting our Father, we learn our chief lesson,
   That our way means failure, and His will is best.

MY SHIP.

Oh, the wonderful things I am going to do,
   And the marvellous visions I cherish,
The works of nobility, world-wide and true,
   The monuments never to perish!
Oh, I will be famous and wealthy and great!
   The bliss of the future is pressing;
I dream of its honours, both early and late,
   When I'll be unto others a blessing.
Yes, I will be noble and learnéd and known,
   Profuse with my money and leisure,
Sought for and honoured, no longer alone,
   When my ship comes home with her treasure.

But while I was dreaming, my ship on the sea
   Was tossed in the water's commotion;
Her sails were all set, she was coming to me
   Across the great boisterous ocean;
But the storm fiercely beat, and she slowly sank low
   To the dirge of the wind's mournful measure;
My dreams have all vanished, I'm bankrupt I know—
   No time and no hope and no treasure.

SILENCE.

There is a time the tongue must powerless fall,
  The soul too full for speech,
When lip to ear has feebly uttered all
  Of love that words can reach ;
Yet heart greets heart with love's peculiar call,
  Dumb language none can teach.

FAITHFUL.

Perhaps we may never lay claim to any grand act heroic,
  Never see ours a great name, or celebrity's banner unfurled,
Yet to do one's duty well is better than martyr or stoic,
  For after all 'tis the little things that make up the life of the world.

Then let us each one do the tasks that to us are given,
  No wasted hours to rue when the sands of our life are run ;
Home, business, profession, toil, can carry the blessing of heaven,
  And he that is "faithful in least" shall be crowned when the race is done.

A QUERY.

Will things go on the same every day,
Will others continue to work and play,
Will the world move on in the same old way,
      When under the sun
      Our life is done ?

Will the seasons change as they used of yore,
Will the sun shine bright as he did before,
Will others live on when our life is o'er ?
      And will they weep
      When we fall asleep ?

Ah, the world moves on in the same old way,
Souls weary, or rested, or sad, or gay.
Whether we go or whether we stay.
      From earth we fly ;
      Our memories die.

One or two hearts alone would mourn,
One or two spirits with grief be torn,
One or two lives be left forlorn
      When we are dead,
      The grasses growing above our head.

CHRIST'S COMING.

It may be at the dawning, at the rosy light of morning,
   That the Master's loving call shall come;
And earth's joys and warfare o'er, we shall sin and weep no more,
   But with Jesus rest forever safe at home.

It may be very soon, at the golden glow of noon,
   That we shall see our Saviour come again.
Echo far and wide the cry, the Bridegroom draweth nigh,
   And our King shall come in majesty to reign.

It may be at evening light, or in the solemn night
   When the silver moon is shining o'er the sea:
We shall share His glory bright, and be clothed in spotless white,
   With Christ, our Lord, forevermore to be.

VANITY.

Vanity, vanity, saith the Preacher,
   Vanity, vanity, all is vain;
And those who glory in vanity's pleasure
   Must likewise suffer with vanity's pain.

THE CHRISTIAN WALK.

1 THESSALONIANS iv. 12, 9, 11, 18, 13, 16.

CHRISTIAN, walk honestly, hold up the cross,
Let not its glory through thee suffer loss;
Its banner thine to keep ever unfurled,
Showing thy colors before a dark world.

Christian, walk lovingly, each man's thy brother;
The Lord hath commanded to "love one another."
Love Christ and give Him all, serve Him for aye,
His love will help thee love those far astray.

Christian, walk carefully, use talents given;
Life work will fit thee for service in heaven;
Time, talent, treasures all, work with thy might,
Do what thy hand can do while it is light.

Christian, walk helpfully, others are weary;
Some hearts are burdened, and some lives are dreary;
Thy hand may ease a load, thy voice may cheer;
Speak, act, and live for men, comfort those near.

Christian, walk hopefully, dread not thy trials,
From out the darkest cloud shine brightest smiles:
Trust in the God of hope, fear not but pray,
After the testing time breaketh the day.

Christian, walk watchfully, thy Lord will come
To take His faithful ones to His fair home;
Those who have followed here there walk forever
In the sweet pastures green by life's clear river.

THE BIBLE.

We prize, we love the precious word,
Our covenant message from our Lord,
Our title-deed to mansions fair,
Our guide to show the pathway there,
Our comforter in time of woe,
Our light to mark the way to go,
Our compass when upon life's sea,
Our friend, our hope where'er we be.

Our standard of a perfect life,
Our sword to conquer in the strife,
Our fund of joy when earth joys fail,
Our source of strength when foes assail,
Our library of knowledge true,
Our help in all we find to do,
Our rock that ever is secure,
Our well of water sweet and pure.

Our treasury that open stands,
A mine of gold beneath our hands;
Our mirror shining clear and bright,
Our shelter from the noonday light,
Our rest when tried with worldly care,
Our song of praise, our word of prayer;
All truths in this old Book combined,
And all who seek shall surely find.

THE GOSPEL.

Jesus died to bring salvation,
   Lasting, full, and free,
Unto every tribe and nation,
   Therefore 'tis for me.

Jesus rose that we might ever
   Know His work complete;
Nothing from His love can sever,
   'Tis assurance sweet.

Dying, risen, living Saviour,
   May we ever be
Working, waiting for Thy favour,
   Faithful unto Thee!

PRAYER.

Prayer is the heart's desire in speech
   Prayer is the wish unspoken,
Prayer is the language of the soul,
   Communion's own love token,
A fellowship of man with God,
   A golden chain unbroken.

MARY AND MARTHA.

Give me the mind of Mary
    To sit at Jesus' feet;
Give me the hands of Martha,
    Busy in service sweet.
Give me the love of Mary,
    Swift to anoint her Lord;
Help me to bring, like Martha,
    The best I can afford.

Give me the heart of Mary,
    The lowliest of the least;
Teach me to work like Martha,
    As servant at the feast.
Oh, may I grow like Mary,
    And choose the better part;
Then toil for Christ like Martha
    In service from the heart.

"HE THAT REGARDETH THE CLOUDS SHALL NOT REAP."

ECCLESIASTES xi. 4.

Sowing the seed in the early dawning,
   In the grey light of the breaking day,
Busily working in life's fair morning,
   Labouring along the appointed way.
Sowing regardless of wind or cloud,
   For in due season the fruit will come,
Garnered in by the Master Reaper,
   Amid the song of the harvest home.

Sowing the seed when the sun is beaming,
   On soil prepared, amid springing flowers;
Sowing the seed when the moonlight gleaming
   With heaven's glory gilds earth's dark hours.
Sowing regardless of wind or cloud,
   For in due season the fruit will come,
Garnered in by the Master Reaper,
   Amid the song of the harvest home.

Sowing the seed in the depths of sorrow,
   In barren ground, or the desert way;
Fearlessly waiting a bright to-morrow,
   For soon shall come the great harvest day.
Sowing regardless of wind and cloud,
   Sowing regardless of shine or storm;
In God's own season the fruit will come,
   What He has promised He will perform.

HIS BANNER.

The banner is unfurled, proclaiming through the world
    The all-atoning sacrifice of Jesus Christ the Son;
And through His precious blood sinners are one with God,
    And share with Him o'er sin and death the victory He
        has won.

The banner is unfurled, proclaiming through the world
    A peace that never endeth, a pardon sealed with blood;
An inheritance above He has purchased by His love,
    And sinners saved by faith in Him are made the heirs
        of God.

The banner is unfurled, proclaiming through the world
    That volunteers are needed in the army of the Lord;
For right shall conquer sin, He shall the battle win,
    In earth and heaven forevermore His name shall be
        adored.

"WITHOUT ME YE CAN DO NOTHING."

JOHN xv. 5.

"WITHOUT Me ye can do nothing." Do we really heed this fact,
That alone, apart from Jesus, worthless is the greatest act?
Men may smile upon our efforts, to our fame their voices raise—
What availeth man's approval if we lack the highest praise?

"Without Me ye can do nothing." Motto for us all along.
He who trusts himself is falling; he who feels his weakness, strong.
"Without Me ye can do nothing!" but "from Me thy fruit is found;"
If our faith were more abiding, then our fruit would more abound.

"Without Me ye can do nothing." This is true, but He is near,
And through Him we "can do all things," and be steadfast without fear.
One with Him, the great Eternal, life divine can never die;
He the source of all fruition and the power to satisfy.

"WHAT SHALL I ASK?"

Mark vi. 34.

"What shall I ask?" The Lord hath said,
　　Whate'er ye ask ye shall receive,
The name of Jesus Christ the plea,
　　The one condition, to believe.
Promises great, I think of this—
Lord, help me not to ask amiss.

"What shall I ask?" For length of days?
　　Ah, no! the future is not mine;
And while I prize the earthly life,
　　I leave its bounds to grace divine.
He who hath made and keeps the soul,
Its destiny will aye control.

"What shall I ask?" A quiet time
　　Of ease, prosperity, and health?
Halcyon days? a paradise?
　　Of this world's goods abundant wealth?
From care and toil complete release,
And over all the wings of peace?

"What shall I ask?" A name and fame
　　That passes down from hand to hand?

The honours of this world all fade,
　　Its names shall perish with its land;
Forgotten (save in memory's love)
Are all but those inscribed above.

"What shall I ask?"　A mind so wise
　　That wisdom is its richest dower?
Or shall I ask for beauty's gift?
　　For grace of face and form are power;
Beauty will fade and reason fail,
The hosts of death will both assail.

"What shall I ask?"　Like he of old,
　　To whom a choice of all was given,
Methinks I will not ask for fame,
　　Nor length of days, but power from heaven
To live so nobly for my King
That He can add every good thing.

And like another saint of old,
　　I'll ask not poverty or gain,
Lest I be rich, forsake my God,
　　Or poor, and take His name in vain;
Content with what His love will give,
Seeking for others' good to live.

I thank Thee for the precious gifts
　　That through Thy grace are showered on me;
Lord, if Thou wilt, let them remain,
　　And they shall still be used for Thee;
For life, and love, and wealth are sweet,
Bestow each as Thou seest meet.

"YE ARE MY WITNESSES."

Have you found Jesus ? Then hasten ye gladly
   Some other wanderer to bring to His feet;
Angels would fain do the work we do sadly,
   Counting both labour and recompense sweet.
Did we but follow our all-loving Saviour,
   Our joy would be greater, our light not so dim ;
We would esteem it a sign of His favor
   That He would let us lead souls unto Him.

PATIENCE AND PERSEVERANCE.

When tasks are hard, and brain is dull, and pulses all aglow,
You long to give the lesson up, the books aside to throw ;
Then plod away, and bear in mind this saying, surely true,
Patience and perseverance will aye see you safely through.

Through all your life 'twill be the same, for earth is but a school,
Lessons to learn, prizes to win, attention to each rule.
Just labour on, for busy hands and hearts are kept from sin ;
Patience and perseverance is the surest way to win.

ANTICIPATION.

We plant a flower and it dies;
We long for a day, lo it flies;
We sigh for a pleasure soon lost,
Gain a treasure, then mourn o'er the cost.

We dread, then we suffer a pain,
Claim a joy, and they're both gone again;
A sorrow we feared is our own,
We pine for to-morrow, 'tis flown

We suffer thus twice
What is past in a trice,
And while troubles tarry
Their burdens we carry,
And lessen the pleasure
And double the pain.

HOME.

What is a home ? Four walls and a roof
    To shelter the folk within ?
Or the loving communion of heart with heart,
    The seclusion of kith and kin ?

Home is the place where we're treated the best,
    And grumble and fret the most ;
Tyrannical, cold to our dearest ones,
    To the stranger a charming host.

But let us beware, for the home life takes
    Our photographs swift and true ;
The polished ones shown to the world, but at home
    The rough negative plates are on view.

For brightness or gloom, for honour or doom,
    None ever can reckon home's worth ;
A cot or a palace, if indwelt by love,
    'Tis the pleasantest place on the earth.

LOOK ON THE BRIGHT SIDE.

THERE'S a bow in every storm if we have but faith to see it,
   There is sunshine for each shadow and refreshing in each shower;
Every cloud is lined with silver, every noontide has its shelter,
   Every desert grows its palm tree, and each barren place its flower.

There is rest for every labour, and a harvest for each sower;
   There's a balm for every pain, and for weakness there is power;
For every leaf that falls there is pledge of life and beauty;
   There is resurrection promise in the fading of each flower.

There's a smile in every tear if the sun but shines upon it,
   There's a calm for every storm, and a star in every night.
So let us learn this lesson, from the daily things around us,
   That sunlight equals shadow when we're looking for the light.

A PATCHWORK QUILT.

" THE light and the dark together, my dear,
    And each one in its place "—
'Twas mother that spake in gentle tone,
    And my work flew on apace.
Black and pink and blue and white,
    Crimson and grey and brown,
Little pieces of this and that,
    And scraps of a worn-out gown.

All dire confusion it looked to me,
    A pattern I could not trace;
But mother knew, so I laboured on,
    Stitching each piece in place.
Odd-shaped fragments of different cloth,
    The dark and the light together;
With never a doubt I worked away
    In sunny or cloudy weather.

So mother planned, and I followed her,
    And my task grew on apace.
How proud I was in my childish glee
    When they all were in their place!—
The labour done, approval won,
    Then I saw the pattern, reaching
O'er more of life than that tiny quilt,
    A deeper lesson teaching;

For life is just like a patchwork quilt,
   Small pieces of light and shade;
But if God plans, and we do our task,
   A beautiful life is made.
The joy, the grief, the work, the rest,
   The bright or cloudy weather,
Will all look right when we see the end,
   The dark and the light together.

A BIRTHDAY.

ANOTHER book of the volume of life
   Is closed and put away,
Till the thoughts of all hearts are open
   In the light of the judgment day.
We fondly glance o'er the faded leaves
   And seal them up with prayer,
And enter upon another year
   With its unknown joy and care.
God grant that none of last year's blots
   May stain the pages fair.

LIFE.

A DAWN of light,
 A morn of bliss,
A noon all bright,
 An evening kiss;
A sunset glow,
 A twilight dim,
A shadow low,
 Thus ends life's hymn.

ABIDING PLACES.

"In my father's house are many abiding places."
—JOHN xiv. 2 (R.V.)

ABIDING places! Can it be
That Jesus has prepared for me
A home, a resting place with Him,
Where truest joys shall never dim—
Abiding place, beyond the range
Of death, of sorrow, or of change?

THE OLD YEAR.

The past has gone forever,
   With its smiles and with its tears,
Its shadow and its sunshine,
   Its trusting and its fears;
Its sorrows and rejoicings,
   Its gaining and its loss,
Its victories and its failures,
   Its comforts and its cross.

The past has gone forever
   With its poverty or wealth,
Its business and its pleasures,
   Its sickness and its health;
Its chances oft neglected,
   Its graces left unwon,
The sins we have committed,
   And the good we've left undone.

The past has gone forever,
   'Twill ne'er return again;
Though fain we would recall it,
   Our efforts are in vain.
Gone to eternal keeping,
   'Tis slumbering but not dead,
And with unerring judgment
   Its record shall be read.

"BEAUTY IS VAIN."

Beauty is charming, and surely will win
  Swift favour in all men's eyes;
Sweetness of feature and grace of form
  Are gifts from God to prize,
Given to few, yet a blessing true
  We never should despise.

But beauty will fade—"'tis but skin deep"—
  And graces and charms will end;
True worth is better, and wealth of mind
  Will greater pleasures lend.
We value a heart and a noble soul,
  Though beauty may not attend.

For "favour's deceitful and beauty is vain,"
  Age will soon lessen their joy;
But "far above rubies" are virtue and love,
  Pure gold without any alloy;
Real goodness is beauty that nothing on earth
  Can ever decrease or destroy.

DISGUISED BLESSINGS.

If we could see beyond the cares oppressing,
   We'd find the very gifts we daily crave;
The heaven-sent cross oft brings an earthly blessing,
   Sweet joys arise to bloom on sorrow's grave.
Beneath our bitter anguish lies the treasure
   We've long years sought, in many ways, in vain;
Our pain is oft the harbinger of pleasure,
   Our losses sometimes prove our truest gain.
Then perish doubt, and hushed be sad complaining;
   For mortal faith is frail and sight is dim;
There's One who rules our lives with love constraining;
   Be still and murmur not, but trust in Him.

NOBILITY.

He is great who doeth daily
   Whatsoe'er his duty be;
He is true who dealeth truly,
   Though no mortal eye may see.
He alone is surely noble
   Who is pure in life and gains,
Though no blood of lord or lady
   Ever flowed within his veins.
He is wise whose mind is duly
   With the highest wisdom stored;
He is rich who wins approval,
   By his fellow-men adored.
He lives long who liveth wisely,
   Though from honour fate debars;
And his standard is too lowly
   Who has aimed beneath the stars.

COMPLAINT.

> "I think we are too ready with complaint
> In this fair world of God's."
> —E. B. Browning.

We are gloomy when we should be joyful,
   Grow weak when we ought to be strong,
Court murmuring in lieu of thanksgiving,
   Choose tear-drops instead of a song.
We complain of the burden or sorrow
   God's providence on us has laid ;
Spoil to-day with dread fears for to-morrow,
   Rejecting the sun for the shade.
Fair, fair is this world God has given,
   His mercies surround all our days ;
Each soul has his portion of heaven,
   Some blessing for which he should praise.

www.ingramcontent.com/pod-product-compliance
Lightning Source LLC
Chambersburg PA
CBHW030309170426
43202CB00009B/937